AF326600

THE
BETTER BOSS
BLUEPRINT

THE BETTER BOSS BLUEPRINT

LIVE AND LEAD WITH #NOREGRETS

SHANI MAGOSKY

PEACH ELEPHANT PRESS

CONTENTS

INTRODUCTION

WELCOME BETTER BOSSES

INTRODUCTION

"The two words information and communication are often used interchangeably, but they signify quite different things. Information is giving out; communication is getting through."
— Sydney Harris, journalist

WELCOME, BETTER BOSSES! You've probably already noticed the nuance in the word choice of "Better" Boss, as opposed to "Perfect" Boss. All bosses are human (at least for the time being!), so perfection is not a realistic goal. Everyone has better boss elements within them already, and we can all be better. A little better today than we were yesterday. A little better tomorrow than we were today. Always learning, growing, and continually improving. What you'll find in this book are lots of practical tips and tools to make that happen—not just the what to do, but just as importantly, the how to do it.

What you'll also find in the book, by way of disclaimer, are mild curse words like asshole and shit. It's not my intention to offend. It's my style to be irreverent, funny, provocative, and direct. Life's too short to beat around the bush. Consistent themes in feedback I receive from clients about working with me in person include "dynamic, creative, insightful, and passionate," and I attempt to bring the same vibe to you in each chapter of this book. That said, if you appreciate a good sense of humor and crave a change from (previously) standard "old, white-guy discourses" on leadership, then welcome to the party!

Welcome to any and all people who crave being better bosses of themselves and others, whether joining us from corporations, start-ups, small business, solopreneurships, non-profits, education, politics, or NGOs. Welcome PTA presidents, sports coaches, and volunteers (lions, tigers, and bears, oh my!). Anywhere there are people, there are bosses to be made better!

Now to get right to the point, per a survey by Lynn Taylor Consulting, a whopping 19.2 hours are wasted each week worrying about what a boss says or does—13 of which occur during the workweek, and 6.2 over the weekend. Can you imagine if people used even a fraction of that time more productively? Furthermore, employee disengagement remains at nearly 70 percent, according to Gallop polls for many years running. Smart people have been writing and speaking about great leadership for decades, yet it doesn't seem to stick. What's out there in leadership content simply isn't working. If it were, we'd be seeing widespread change happening within organizations.

In my opinion, there is too much focus on the symptoms of workplace dysfunction rather than on the underlying diseases causing it—disconnected relationships and a lack of transparent communication. Being successful at work is ultimately a choice every person must make for him or herself, irrespective of any formal training provided by employers. That's why The Better Boss Project was created: to provide tools for Living and Leading with #NoRegrets that are accessible for anyone who is willing to be proactive in "treating" the diseases they encounter at work and in life.

Why the #NoRegrets piece? Let's examine an official definition of the word:

> Regret, verb | re·gret | \ri-'gret\ a feeling of sadness or disappointment about something that you did or did not do

Who isn't all in for a lower quotient of sadness and disappointment! For now, suffice it to say that the genesis and significance of #NoRegrets to better boss behavior will become imminently clear in the subsequent `pages.

The Better Boss Project is a movement directed at organizations and individuals worldwide to enroll, inspire, and equip people to be better bosses not only of other people, but also of themselves. It's a mindset held by people who take personal responsibility for their leadership style and career success. It cuts through the BS, clutter, and complex messages in the leadership development world and aims to infuse humanity and actual conversation back into the workplace. Yes, those are good intentions in and of themselves. But also, from a practical business standpoint, it will drive improved:

› Relationships
› Communication
› Cultural dynamics
› Engagement
› Teamwork and co-creation
› Accountability

› Productivity and innovation
› Ability to manage change
› Retention of best talent
› Business and financial results
› Abundance that gets shared

GREAT BOSSES AT GOLDMAN SACHS

When I first moved to New York City after college, a lot of my friends were working as financial analysts in investment banks. Of course, they were working their asses off—long days, most nights, and virtually every weekend—but it seemed extremely stimulating and glamorous. They got to fly around the country, if not the world, attend meetings with CEOs and CFOs, and work on important deals...it just seemed like the dream to me. I was working at Chase Manhattan Bank at the time and thought to myself, "If they can do it, I can do it. I don't care that they have Ivy League degrees and I don't." I was valedictorian of my class in the School of Communication at the University of Miami. I was just as smart as they were, and I could do that job too!

So I started applying for analyst positions at all the big investment banks. Goldman Sachs, my first choice, was also my first offer. I was placed into the Energy & Power group (E&P), which essentially serves oil and gas companies and utilities. Finance in general is a male-dominated industry, but boy, the oil and gas business takes testosterone to a whole different level.

But my experience was an extraordinary one, thanks to a better boss.

The leader of the E&P group at Goldman was a guy named David Leuschen, a fifth-generation Montana man with a big stature and an even bigger personality. He came from a good family, but you would not necessarily have imagined him choosing an investment banking career. Most of the people who make it big on Wall Street are not fifth-generation Montana cowboy types, you know? But it worked for him.

He was larger than life for me. He created a culture in E&P that was second to none in all of the Investment Banking Division (IBD)—we became famous for working hard and playing hard.

And, let me emphasize that, as analysts (the most junior bankers on the totem pole), we did work really f**king hard. We drove ourselves seven days a week, including nights and weekends. We pulled all-nighters. I literally did not take a day off for the entire first year I worked at Goldman. That was just fine with me, because I was learning so much. It was like a high-speed train of business experience, and I wouldn't trade it for anything. Let's be honest—if you're going to have the energy for that, it'll be in your early and mid-20s.

Every week, we had Monday morning meetings for which the entire E&P group would congregate in a large conference room, and get this—the more tenured folks actually cared about what the analysts had to say! We were doing all the financial modeling, analytical, and PowerPoint work for pitches and deals, as well as writing first drafts of internal docs for the commitments committee, investment committee, and equity or fixed income salesforces. Not only were we encouraged to actively participate in these internal meetings, but also, we were invited to virtually all client meetings. If the client had questions on any of the Excel spreadsheets, for example, the senior bankers would look to us for answers. We were a team, and that experience was invaluable. Sitting in meetings with CEOs, CFOs, heads of this, and heads of that, you learn at a very early stage in your

In my cubicle on the 23rd floor of Goldman's 85 Broad Street headquarters. The hard hat is a vestige of a deal I worked on advising French oil company Elf Aquitaine on the sale of a mining subsidiary. You've got to love the enormous computer with dual floppy disk drives!

career how relationships work and how great minds think about putting deals together. When we look back, for many of us, it was a favorite time in our careers.

To say I worked with the best and brightest is an understatement. In fact, some of the highest quality people, on both a professional and personal level, with whom I have ever worked, were from my IBD days at Goldman. IBD people were generous with their time for mentoring and developing each other, from my fellow analysts all the way up to the most senior partners. Integrity, intense focus, and clear communication were hallmark virtues of IBD that rubbed off on all of us in that era. These are values I have carried with me to every subsequent job, and throughout life in general, with great success. And now to The Better Boss Project.

This book is full of stories about other bosses I've had over the years who were great, and some who maybe weren't so great. In addition, I openly share personal experiences of being a boss I was proud of and experiences in which I wasn't such a "better boss." As with anything, I've learned as much by doing as I have by watching.

I never lost touch with my first "Better Boss" at Goldman Sachs, David Leuschen. This was taken at a E&P reunion event in 2013.

MEETING ALAN

My very first roommate in New York was an awesome woman named Wendy. We had an absolute blast together as friends and party buddies. One Saturday night, she wanted me to go out with her, but I really wasn't in the mood—maybe I was tired, maybe I wasn't feeling well, I can't remember—but she was insistent. She pretty much dragged me out with her to a bar on the Upper West Side of Manhattan called The Black Bass, where she coincidentally ran into an old friend from high school. While Wendy and Adam were catching up, I started talking to Adam's (very cute) friend and medical school roommate, Alan. I'll never forget this—at the end of the night, Alan asked, "Can I have your phone number?"

"Sure," I said. "Let's find something to write on." I started to look for a pen, but he insisted, "Oh, no need to write it down. I'll remember it."

"Yeah, right," I laughed.

"No, really," he said. "I'm a med student. That's what I do. I memorize things."

I humored him and recited my number, but I never expected to actually get a call from Alan.

As you might have guessed, I did get a call. He remembered. We had our first date the following weekend, on Halloween, and were inseparable after that.

What an interesting night our first date was! He took me to a Caribbean restaurant downtown, because he knew I had gone to college in Miami and surely must like Caribbean food. After dinner, we went to Greenwich Village for the infamous Halloween parade and ultimately ended up at the Back Fence,

One of my all-time favorite photos of Alan and me. This was taken at a party celebrating his graduation from Mount Sinai Medical School in 1994.

one of my favorite bars in NYC because of the great music and laid-back atmosphere with peanut shells on the ground.

A friendly, very new-age-ish woman in flowing bohemian clothing and lots of gold jewelry sat alone at a table to our right. As God is my witness, this lady turned to us right out of the gate and asked, "How long have you two been married?" We giggled and informed her that not only were we not married, but it was also our first date. She couldn't believe it, convinced us to let her read our palms, and insisted that we were to be married.

Alan and I eventually moved in together in a building on the Upper East Side near Mount Sinai Hospital, where he would be doing his general surgery residency, and I commuted all the way downtown to Goldman Sachs. My Energy & Power colleagues all knew and loved Alan. The vice presidents used to host these huge parties to which spouses and kids were invited, so we got to know each other's loved ones. It felt like a really big family, and Alan was a part of it.

It was during Alan's second year of residency that he started having a lot of back pain. He ignored it for a long time. Too long. He figured it was his crazy and physically demanding work schedule—he was on his feet all day in surgeries, on call multiple nights a week, either not sleeping or sleeping on uncomfortable cots in the call room. He self-medicated with Advil and did what he had to do.

This went on for months, as he refused to go see a doctor about it. Doctors are notoriously the worst patients. He's a tough guy, so he wanted to tough it out. But when the pain started moving down his hips and legs, I'd had enough of his being some hero doctor; it was time to see an orthopedist.

By this time, I had moved from investment banking to the fixed-income trading floor in the High Yield group (referred to in the biz as "the high yield desk"), where I worked from 1995 through 2000. It was an incredibly exciting time to be part of the high yield business, because we were not only doing deals for industrial companies, which had previously been the bread and butter, but we were also starting to finance start-ups, telecom companies, and other hot, emerging businesses. It was fun, and I loved the variety! In any given week, we might be doing deals for a cable company, global satellite startup, a steel or mining company, oil driller, casino, media stalwart, old-line manufacturer, retail empire, or internet wunderkind.

It was while I was on the desk one otherwise insignificant day that I got the call telling me Alan had been admitted to the hospital. That really surprised me. I just figured he'd go have some tests run, and some smart doctor would figure out what it was, fix it, and his pain would go away.

Unfortunately, that's not what happened. After a series of tests, they found mysterious lesions on his bones.

Alan was in the hospital for a good week before they finally identified the source of his back pain and those lesions: stage four, metastatic colon cancer. It had started in a polyp on his colon and then spread throughout his body. The crazy thing was his colon didn't present with much cancer; rather, a lymph vessel in the polyp had spread the cancer throughout his body in an unusually quick way. The pain was driven by metastases on his bones ("bone mets"). It was not muscle or joint pain. It was bone pain, which takes agony to a whole different level. Likely, it had spread elsewhere as well.

He was twenty-seven years old, and I was twenty-six. As you can imagine, the last piece of news we were expecting was a fatal cancer diagnosis. Alan started chemotherapy, but from the very beginning, the oncologist told us it wasn't a cure. It could only slow the progression of the cancer so he would (maybe) have a little bit more time.

I vividly remember the afternoon sitting in Alan's hospital room when we got the devastating diagnosis. After speaking with the doctors, I called my boss, Barbara Tartell, from a pay phone (this was a couple of years before Blackberries were standard issue on Wall Street). I was in tears, sharing that Alan had just been diagnosed with stage four cancer, and her reaction couldn't have been more kind and empathetic.

First of all, I could hear that she was also tearing up. Barbara is a mother of three children, and what I had just shared with her was every mother's worst nightmare. She told me my priority should be taking care of Alan, being with Alan, having no regrets, not worrying about work. "Come into work when you want to," she said. "Don't come in when you can't. Just keep in touch, and we'll figure this out."

Her reaction was such a relief. Here I was, less than a year into my new role, in a job that most MBA students would have probably cut off an arm to be offered at that time, and my boss had my back. It was amazing. What's more, the person to whom Barbara reported, Jon Winkelried, reinforced the message of support from Barbara and the firm. I had the support of my boss and my boss's boss. Clearly, my time there was marked by good fortune in having such fantastic leaders. I couldn't have done it without the flexibility and kindness they extended. Believe me, there were other managers at the firm who wouldn't have cared much and would likely have told me, "Tough situation, but figure out how to deal with it." Thankfully, I didn't have bosses like that, and it made a lifelong impression on me about the importance of empathy and treating people as you would want to be treated.

Before all this happened, all I wanted was to be a partner at Goldman Sachs. I was singularly focused on my job. I definitely have regrets about time I didn't spend with Alan before he was diagnosed, because I often chose work over him. I chose work over everything and anything else, frankly. Along the way, we

My better boss, Barbara Tartell, whose empathy and support saved my sanity during and after Alan's battle with cancer. This picture from the early-mid 1990s captures Barbara in her element, a female powerhouse on the male-dominated Fixed Income trading floor at Goldman Sachs.

had gotten engaged, but never got married because "we didn't have time." Little did we know.

But after he was diagnosed, there was nothing more important to me than making sure he had everything he needed to be comfortable. Although he received first-class care at Mount Sinai Hospital, Alan preferred to be home in our apartment when his condition would allow for it. I became his nurse and primary caregiver. The hospital staff taught me how to administer his chemotherapy into the catheter implanted in his chest. They educated me about all the other medications he was on—and there were a lot. He was in and out of the hospital with all kinds of complications for about seven months, until he passed away in our apartment on July 25, 1996. When the Dixie Chicks song "Cold Day in July" came out a few years later in 1999, I thought it had been written for me.

The #NoRegrets piece of The Better Boss Project motto should be making sense right about now, if it hasn't already.

I was out of the office for about two weeks of "formal" mourning, with Alan's family in New York for the first week, and then I went home to my family in South Florida for the second week. When I got back to work, I threw myself back into it like I had nothing else.

Honestly, at that time, I didn't really think I did have anything else.

Everyone loved Alan. Even my childhood dog Hawkeye wanted to go home with Alan at the end of a visit we made to see my family in Florida.

LEAVING GOLDMAN SACHS

The downside, of course, to throwing myself exclusively into my work was that I never effectively dealt with the grief. Several years went by during which I couldn't get rid of the intense anger and bitterness about my situation. I grew more senior at work, with increasing responsibility, bigger clients, and expectations to match. One of my new clients was a total asshole, and I took his actions very personally—which I now know not to do—but at the time, it was quite anxiety-provoking. To top it all off, I was recovering from a skiing accident and battling a chronic sinus infection. Stress piled on top of unprocessed rage was a recipe for a ticking time bomb.

I was, to say the least, pretty worn down. And severely pissed off at the world.

This weariness and dejection started to show in my demeanor. Before, even in the years immediately after Alan's death, I had always been known as an ebullient culture-carrier at Goldman. I loved recruiting and was consistently tapped to lead training programs for new hires or be the liaison for summer MBA students. I had always eagerly stepped into those kinds of extracurricular roles because I had such boundless enthusiasm and loyalty to the firm. So when my disposition darkened, it was very noticeable.

Jon Winkelried, or "Winks" as we called him, pulled me off the trading floor into a conference room one day, and in the most authentic, compassionate way, he opened the conversation with a simple question.

"What is going on with you?" There was no judgment, no assumptions, no accusations. The question was full of sincerity and kindness—he really wanted to know what was happening.

"Do you really want to know?" I asked.

"Of course, I want to know," he replied, and I promptly broke down into tears (something I had never done at work). I explained everything that was going on: personal life, work stressors, the douchebag client, health challenges, the whole shit show. Then, he did the best thing I think any boss could have done in that situation—he insisted I take a vacation. He didn't mean eventually go on holiday; he meant ASAP and joked that he'd toss me out of the building if I showed up in the office the following week. If hashtags had been a thing back then, it could have been the first-known use of #kiddingnotkidding.

I left a few days later for Capri, Italy, headed to a spa to pamper myself for a solid week. Uncharacteristically, I started journaling while I was there, really trying to figure out what was up and what would really make me happy. I took the time to ask myself some important existential questions that you don't really have a chance to ask yourself when you work in a very demanding job, and I came to some important conclusions.
The decision I made during that vacation altered the course of my career and the rest of my life. I decided to leave NYC. I had an epiphany that the major reason I wasn't healing was because New York was constantly rubbing salt in the wound. You see, virtually everything about NYC reminded me of Alan. Furthermore, I couldn't separate my job from the city where Wall Street made its home, so I decided Goldman was a related source of oppression. Soon thereafter, I got a job offer from one of my favorite clients in Los Angeles. When I resigned from

Goldman in January 2000, Jon and others wished me the best and said I'd be welcome back any time.

On a side note, Jon had a huge career at Goldman, and by the time he retired, he was Co-President of the firm. So it's unlikely he remembers any of this. Better bosses never know the impact they can have on others. It's what Drew Dudley calls a "lollipop moment" in his TED Talk "Everyday Leadership"—situations in which we impact someone's life for the better, usually without even realizing it.

It seemed like the right decision at the time, but what I realize in hindsight is that it had nothing to do with New York or Goldman. It had everything to do with me. Hold that thought for later.

A NEW KIND OF MANAGEMENT

A lot happened after that, but here's the Reader's Digest version: I moved to Santa Monica, California, bought a frivolous convertible, made some amazing friends, took up rock climbing, and smiled more. I quit the job there after one year, and then spent another year traveling the world. I met my husband Brad while on the South Island of New Zealand, moved in with him in Chicago, got married, and even worked for Goldman Sachs again, this time in the Equities division. But it was moving to Vail, Colorado that I see as the next significant step towards The Better Boss Project.

Initially, I had a hard time finding a position in Vail; there aren't a lot of senior level management positions in a tourist town. Then I was introduced to the interim general manager of the (then) brand-new TV station in town, Plum TV, aka "Plum."

Posing with Brad at one of many hiking trailheads. We were inseparable once we met at the Christchurch, New Zealand airport.

The key word here is "interim," as in they were on the hunt for a full-time, local replacement. The East Coast-based president of Plum came to town to interview candidates, and when I entered the conference room, it was clear he hadn't looked at my resume in advance. He finally looked up at me with a confused look on his face and asked, "What are you doing here? Why is a Wall Streeter interviewing for a TV station manager job?"

I explained to him that I was switching careers and felt very confident I had the transferable skills to do the job. By the end of the interview, he concluded it would be a lot easier to teach me the nuts and bolts of the television industry than to teach a creative, producer-type how to run a business. I got the job offer, and it turned out to be a great experience—not only because it diversified my resume away from financial services,

After meeting Brad in New Zealand, I traveled around Thailand for a month before returning home to L.A. Here, I'm celebrating the completion of my first ever multi-pitch climb, led by a friendly local rock climbing guide named Gop.

but also because it illuminated many valuable contrasts between working at a startup versus a very established business.

We never had enough budget or staff, whereas at Goldman we had any resources ever needed. I worked with very right-brained, creative types at Plum, as opposed to the logical, linear, left-brained sorts on Wall Street. At Goldman, I worked with people of multiple generations, whereas the large majority of my staff at Plum were millennials right out of college. Most importantly, at the TV station, I couldn't just be a manager; I also had to be a leader.

While in a manager role at Goldman, I could tell people what to do, when to do, how to do, and with whom to do—because I had done their jobs. I had come up through the system. I had been in more junior roles and knew the various products and services in different divisions as well as different client types, so I could just pontificate to junior people to help bring them up to speed. At Plum, I couldn't do that. I didn't know how to instruct video editors on Final Cut Pro. I didn't know how to produce television shows. Therefore, a much different approach to leading was called for; I had to inspire and empower people to do what they did best.

The results were phenomenal. By the end of our first year, we were nominated for the Best New Business Award by the Vail Chamber of Commerce and received runner-up. It was very validating of the tremendous effort we had all put forth and the buzz we had created in town. We had gotten the community

Adorning an old chairlift with my amazing Plum TV crew on the patio of our offices in West Vail.

enthusiastic, which was essential, since they were the ones interacting with tourists and recommending which local station to watch!

A JOKE IN THE PAPER

One morning, I was having coffee and flipping through the Vail Daily newspaper. As I paged through the classifieds, an ad stuck out to me because it was in bold, all capital letters.

"ARE YOU AN EAST COAST PERSON, WITH EAST COAST WORK ETHIC, AND EAST COAST WORK EXPERIENCE, BUT YOU LIVE IN THE MOUNTAINS FOR LIFESTYLE REASONS? AND DO YOU HAVE EXPERIENCE WITH FINANCE, HUMAN RESOURCES, AND OPERATIONS?"

Was this a joke?

I didn't yet know what the company was, but the job sure sounded perfect for me. I applied, interviewed, and received an offer during the interview. I was now Chief Operating Officer of a B2B marketing and public relations company, one that the owner had recently taken from a brick-and-mortar business in Washington, D.C. to an all-virtual company. He had already been frequenting his second home in Colorado, and finally gave up the expensive real estate on Pennsylvania Avenue, sent everybody home with computers, and saved a ton of overhead. Then, when he moved to Colorado full time, he quickly realized he wanted to ski, play more golf, and enjoy the fruits of his labor—so he sought someone to be his Number Two.

I fit that bill and did a lot of different things for the business. There was remarkable learning for me, in particular on the IT side. For example, we needed the right technology to support productivity, collaboration, communication, knowledge sharing, and document storage for our highly-distributed team. I immediately educated myself on areas I never really had to think about previously, and one of the first things I did was migrate us off what was an old Microsoft terminal server and onto the cloud. We were very early adopters of cloud computing, and the decision proved to be hugely beneficial.

After almost five years, I felt as though I'd grown the company as far as I could grow it within the confines of the owner's vision. I had operationalized everything to a point of excellence; we had a great team, we had stable customers, and I was ready to move on.

By that point, I had collected a unique and rare set of experiences and expertise from having worked in different industries, across a variety of functional areas, leading different types of people, and in different geographies and economic climates. I was confident that I could once again do something new. This time, my sights were set upon leadership development, employee engagement, and talent management consulting and coaching.

COACHING AND BEYOND

When I was contemplating leaving Goldman Sachs, I hired an executive coach to help me figure out "what I wanted to be when I grow up." It was incredibly helpful to work with this coach to get more in touch with what fulfilled me, motivated me, and made me happy. Between that experience and my time leading the TV station, I knew coaching was a profoundly valuable leadership competency, and I wanted to make a living doing and teaching it.

I enrolled in a coach training and certification program at the gold-standard Coaches Training Institute (CTI). During those eighteen months back in school, so to speak, I started the predecessor business to The Better Boss Project, Vitesse Consulting. Vitesse is the blend of "vitality" and "success," two things I felt everybody wanted. It's also the French word for "speed"—which is a great double entendre, given the head-spinning pace at which we work today.

Eventually, I wanted to make a bigger impact than I could via individual coaching and consulting gigs. I learned, from so many of my personal experiences, what a difference a great boss can make. A boss can define the whole culture of a company and impact endless lives. We don't just need consultants; we need better boss ubiquity! Thus, The Better Boss Project was born.

WHAT DOES A BAD BOSS LOOK LIKE?

Sadly, there are more bad bosses out there than better bosses. Some are just overtly bad managers—out for themselves, not team players, only concerned about how they look, and/or in self-preservation mode. They don't communicate effectively, they give as well as receive feedback defensively, and often act passive-aggressively. They can't get their heads out of their own asses long enough to lead people in an effective way.

Some bad bosses are less insidious. They might not even realize the impact they're having on other people. They're fearful, not self-aware, don't know what they don't know, haven't dealt with their own weaknesses, haven't educated themselves, haven't had good role models—you name it. They don't mean to be bad bosses, but their behaviors are disempowering to their people nevertheless.

Bad bosses micromanage because they can't let go. They don't delegate, but instead take on other people's projects and, therefore, they don't devote enough time to their own goals and miss strategic opportunities. Personal lives suffer, and health probably suffers too, because they're taking on too much—just working more hours instead of working smarter.

THE VICIOUS CYCLE OF BAD BOSSES

The team loses motivation under the leadership of bad bosses, which makes for unfortunate consequences and poor relationships. It gets hard to not become resentful when you're trying to do everything and your team just isn't performing. It becomes a self-reinforcing loop—your team isn't performing, so you do more of what made them not perform in the first place, which is even more disempowering for them, which causes them to perform even less, and it becomes more frustrating for you, and so on. It's a vicious cycle, because you can't get what you need out of your team. Nobody's happy. Nobody's motivated. Those employees certainly won't ever go the extra mile. They're easily distracted. They'll spend time gossiping and complaining instead of actually being productive. They're probably already looking for another job; they're not loyal, because there's no trust or good faith to keep them committed.

Innovation doesn't happen here, because it's not considered safe to fail. No one is motivated to take things to the next step, let alone to the next level, because they're used to creative ideas being shot down or discouraged.

For anyone who isn't a sociopath, it doesn't feel good to be a bad boss! It's stressful. Who wants to come home from work feeling as if they've let others down? As if they didn't do their best? As if they should have handled things differently?

PEOPLE ARE ASSETS!

Managing people is the hardest part of being a boss. It's not straightforward. It's not just about executing; there's also emotion, human dynamics, group subtleties, and politics at work. There are all sorts of exogenous factors, not to mention assorted distractions trying to steal your focus. To make matters worse, too often employees are promoted to managerial positions because they're great at their job. But those skills don't necessarily transfer. Great engineers, attorneys, and salespeople doesn't necessarily have leadership qualifications, but they're advanced to those jobs anyway. Historically, not enough companies have invested in training new managers or in ongoing management skills and leadership development. Sadly, those were, and often still are, seen as "soft skills" that don't generate quantifiable returns.

We assert that there is an invaluable return on great leadership! It's a relatively new phenomenon for companies to view people as assets. Historically, assets were defined as manufacturing plants and other tangible possessions, but our economy transitioned years ago to knowledge and services.

Organizations are finally learning to treat people like assets and to invest in those assets to develop better bosses.

LEADERSHIP MINDSET: THE BETTER BOSS PROJECT

The Better Boss Project is an investment in people. It isn't just a company or project; it's a mindset that can apply to any organization, in any country, in any industry, no matter how big or small. It's a movement with a shared language. We can all be better every single day. We must be more cognizant of the impact we have on other people. It's about taking a moment to pause before we react—because there are certain things we can't take back or do over. It's about building new muscle memory around what good leadership looks like. It's a shift in perspective.

This book aims to deliver some concrete tools—of both the "art" and "science" variety—to help you adopt such a mindset. The chapters are based on ten commitments that propel better bosses to success, which we call The Better Boss Blueprint. I'll be the first to admit I'm a little acronym-happy, and many of the tools for how to be a better boss are presented in the form of clever acronyms. It's challenging for adults to learn and adopt new habits, so the acronyms are merely mnemonic devices to make it as easy as possible to remember the concepts.

TO THE READER

You have the potential to be a better boss. If you want to make a change, you must take the first step. Or you can continue to operate the old way at your own risk. Like anything else, I don't expect you to buy into everything you read here. If there are certain aspects of The Better Boss Project that resonate more than others, great! Latch on to those. For anything you feel particularly ambivalent about, consider asking yourself why. What about it triggers you? There's a reason you're resistant, and it will probably be better for you in the long run if you understand why.

Either way, take something from this book. Make a change to be a better boss, and watch the ripple effects on your team, in your workplace, and in your world.

ONE

[As a Better Boss, I commit to:]

WORK CONTINUOUSLY ON HAVING MY OWN SHIT TOGETHER

ONE

[As a Better Boss, I commit to:]

WORK CONTINUOUSLY ON HAVING MY OWN SHIT TOGETHER

"Becoming a leader is synonymous with becoming yourself. It is precisely that simple and also that difficult. First and foremost, find out what it is you're about and be that."
– Warren Bennis, On Becoming a Leader

BOSSES, LISTEN UP: It's hard to help other people be better at what they do if you're a f**king mess. The universal flight attendants' script instructs passengers that if an airplane crashes, put on your own oxygen mask first, because you're useless to anyone else if you're not breathing. Similarly, if you want to be a good leader, you've got to have your own house in order. If you're not aware of your own bad habits, it's going to be hard to cascade good habits or expect them of your team.

Getting your shit together means taking time to focus on three primary points. First, focus on the big picture. *Start with your values*—those are foundational. Then *deal with the fears* that hold you back. Thirdly, *take care of yourself.*

START WITH VALUES

Values are ways of operating in life that help guide our behaviors, thoughts, and decision-making processes. They're filters through which we look at life. Values are like the North Star; when we're lost, we can zone in on our values—they should always be in the same place.

Values help create who we are in our own uniqueness. They're what get us out of bed every morning to do what we do. That's part of what we seek in our experiences—to honor our values every single day. We can't build healthy lives, careers, or relationships if we don't have a solid foundation of personal and professional values.

You know you're out of alignment with your values if you're really unhappy. For example, if you're miserable in a job, figure out which one of your values is being threatened or downright trampled. Discovering that will open up all kinds of possibilities and opportunities for change.

Typical values most people think of are ones like honesty, integrity, hard work, etc. Those are great, but values can represent so much more; they can be so much more specific and original. For example, one of my values is rock climbing, which may sound really odd to some people. "No, Shani, rock climbing isn't a value, it's a sport—a scary sport." But for me, rock climbing represents freedom, adventure, the outdoors, fresh air, and meditation. I hold it very dearly. When I'm up on a rock face (on belay of course!), my mind is so focused on the granite or sandstone puzzle that's in front of me that the rest of the world is completely tuned out. It's the clearest state I ever summon. Rock climbing is an umbrella designation capturing a cluster of related values for me.

Get creative with your values. Name them anything—a sport, person, place, object, a dream, a made-up word—whatever starts that fire in you. Attach resonant identities to your North Star.

FINDING YOUR VALUES

How can you do that? How can you, dearest Better Boss reader, discover your values?

There are a lot of ways to go about this. You could just sit down and brainstorm them on a piece of paper. You could go to a website of values and pick the ones that ring true for you. When I work with clients, I prefer to ask them a litany of provocative questions. Then, I listen carefully to glean what values show up in their answers—even unintentionally. Typically, the first query is this: "Fast-forward twenty years from now. Imagine that you're being honored at a big event. You're being given a lifetime achievement award. What's the award for?"

"Now, imagine the person who's introducing you at this ceremony, the person who will bestow this award upon you. What is he/she saying about you? What are the highlights of his/her speech? What stood out in your accomplishments?" The answers people give provide considerable insight into their value structures.

A simpler question is the age-old "What would you do if you won the lottery?" Other personal favorites are "What can't you tolerate?", "Who is your role model and what about that person do you admire?", and "If you could have one superpower, what would it be and why?" The answers to questions like these give us clues to what we value most.

When I pose these questions to clients, I'm looking for what's underneath their answers. I'm listening for *why* they're answering this way; what's important to them? You can do the same for yourself. Are your answers achievement-oriented and ambitious? It's likely that being challenged is a precious value. Do your answers revolve around your children or spouse? If so, the value of family relationships shines through.

WHY VALUES MATTER

If you don't know what your values are, you're just going to randomly wander through life. Values define who we are, where we're going, and why we make the choices we do. None of us want to think we're here to just go through the motions. We're here for a purpose, on a small scale or on a large scale. Get in touch with why you're doing things, and why those things matter—therein lies your purpose.

When we live life outside of the perimeters of our values, we feel dissonance. It feels wrong, it feels off, and if we don't identify what our values are, we may never be able to put a finger on exactly why we're feeling shitty. Another one of my core values is health and wellness. Occasionally in my life, when my career gets too demanding, I end up eating poorly, I stop exercising, and/or I don't get enough sleep. As a result, I feel dreadful and severely unhappy, but I know exactly why: because I've stopped honoring that health and wellness value (not to mention the rock climbing value!).

Similarly, if you value creativity or have an insatiable thirst for new knowledge and find yourself in a very monotonous job, boredom is going to eat you alive unless you make a change. If you value independence and accountability but work for a micromanager, you likely hate your job. It doesn't have to just be in your career though. In any aspect of your life, if you get that pit in your stomach, or your heart starts to race, or you physically feel unsettled, then you know whatever you've just done is not in line with your values. Your body reacts; you feel like shit! If you don't know what your values are, you'll have a much more difficult time getting back on track.

Knowing your values can also lead you directly to knowing your purpose and vision. Imagine it as a funnel: once you confirm your values, then you can drill down to figure out your larger purpose. Is it to invent something future generations will still utilize? Is it to be a great parent and valued family member? Is it to serve underprivileged youth? Is it to make a mark in politics? Is it to spend as much time as you can exploring the world? Then, as you delve into your own psyche, you can uncover even more detail and develop a long-term vision for how to fulfill that purpose. Go deeper still, and you'll reach ground level—where you take action on it.

BEAUTY IS NOT THE ONLY THING IN THE EYE OF THE BEHOLDER (I.E. BE AWARE OF YOUR FILTERS)

As you discover your values, it's important to recognize that every value you hold and every experience you have in life combine to form your personalized filters, which I like to describe as the prescription in the pair of glasses through which only you look at the world. Of course, filters generate unconscious biases, just as looking through sunglasses or ski goggles tinted in black, brown, rose, green, or yellow will generate slightly different images of what's in front of us. These aren't necessarily good or bad, but they certainly affect our perspective. We all grow up with certain influences that shape who we are. Values are a big part of that, and so are a lot of other factors: parents, teachers, friends, past employment, religion, local customs, native language, and geographic setting, to name a few.

The filters that form from these experiences are unique to us; no one else will share the exact same lens. Part of understanding your values involves recognizing what's in that lens—why might you be inclined to make certain judgments or assumptions? This can be as easy as taking a moment to reflect.

If you catch yourself assuming, don't necessarily judge it or yourself—instead, notice it and explore where it came from. Make that a practice. For example, you might reflect, "I just assumed that Pam isn't returning my phone call because she's annoyed with me, or she's not interested in the product that I'm selling. But I don't know for sure that's true, I just assume it is." Once you recognize the assumption, you also realize you have no earthly idea why Pam didn't call back. But the fact that you leapt to conclusions can teach you a lot about yourself. Maybe you have a value of dependability or reliability; you're the type who always responds when you get an email or phone call. Or maybe you have a belief based on a prior experience. "When Jake didn't call me back, it was because he wasn't interested." But that doesn't mean that's the case now. When you dismantle your assumptions, more peace and ease naturally follow!

Being curious about your own mind to understand where your assumptions come from is the first step towards taking their power away. And then, guess what, you'll have fewer regrets!

WHAT ARE YOU AFRAID OF?

The second important element of getting your own shit together, after deciphering your values, filters, and assumptions, is battling your fears. Fear is the single biggest saboteur to success. Think of any critical voice you hear in the back of your mind; it's most likely rooted in fear. Fear of failure, fear of success, fear of looking bad, fear of looking good, fear of not being enough, fear of being too much, fear of taking action, fear of not taking action, fear of not being liked, fear of being too well-liked, fear of the future, fear of the past. FOMO (Fear Of Missing Out). Fear of crowds, fear of being alone. Recognize any of yours?

Journalist and author Dan Harris described that fear-mongering internal voice in a way that nearly made my side split from laughter. The opening lines of his book *10% Happier* read, "I initially wanted to call this book *The Voice in My Head is an Asshole*. However, that title was deemed inappropriate for a man whose day job requires him to abide by FCC decency standards." As the beautifully articulated rampage continues, he portrays this internal narrator as "the voice that comes braying in as soon as we open our eyes in the morning and then heckles us all day long with an air horn. It's a fever swamp of urges, desires, and judgments."

Here's a cool perspective I once heard about F.E.A.R.: It is Fantasy and Expectations Appearing Real. We create it ourselves, in our own heads. We make assumptions and believe the stories emanating from those assumptions.

Fear is a reactive, rather than a thoughtful and intentional, way to engage with the world. How you react when you're afraid tells you a lot about what your fears mean and how they manifest.

- › Do you shift into people-pleasing mode, seeking to be the center of attention or trying to get everyone to like you?
- › Do you remain passive or attempt to become one with the wallpaper, not wanting to rock the boat?
- › Do you deflect, blame, and overly criticize others to make yourself feel better?
- › Do you try to control everyone and everything?

These seemingly disparate reactions have something in common: they are all defense mechanisms in response to fear.

Everyone's had bosses who fit one or more of those profiles. Any such extreme reactive behaviors will hinder effective leadership. Let's examine them one at a time, using some playfully exaggerated archetypes.

The People-Pleaser: First, nobody's going to like the boss all the time. If you try to please everybody, you're going to please nobody. "I can't give you a sure-fire formula for success, but I can give you a formula for failure: try to please everybody all the time," said Pulitzer Prize-winning journalist Herbert Bayard Swope. An antidote to this style is anchoring yourself in the values, purpose, and vision we explored earlier when making decisions, solving problems, and taking action.

The Wallpaper: This type of boss habitually goes along to get along and rarely, if ever, speaks up or acts on leadership urges. How can you make a real impact as a leader if you fade into the woodwork, let people walk all over you, or don't show up at all?

The Arrogant Prick/Bitch: These bosses tend to pump themselves up by knocking others down. They typically foster an unrealistic culture where perfect is the enemy of the great, as they say. No failure, of any magnitude, is tolerated. But as filmmaker James Cameron said, "Failure has to be an option. No important endeavor that required innovation was done without risk." When people are afraid of constant criticism or extreme consequences of failure, some may even lie or hide the truth, adding insult to injury for the organization.

The Tyrant: It's "my way or the highway" with such bosses who try to control everything. They are the micromanagers, often the ones with zero respect for their own or others' personal lives, and can be some of the most blood sucking, morale-destroying managers around. They tend to have high turnover among their best performers—a ramification with nearly unquantifiable cost.

It's hard to see bosses or individual contributors as trusted, capable, or competent when they're engaging in fear-based behaviors.

STOP WAITING FOR CONFIDENCE

Confidence comes after you succeed, not before—so stop waiting for it to arrive in some sort of metaphysical little blue Tiffany's box. If you're waiting for confidence to act, you're going to be waiting all day. It's not until after you give it a whirl and actually succeed that your confidence builds. So take that first step—any first step!

Just as with values, analyzing your fears is about asking questions. If you notice you're afraid, stop and take stock. What are you really scared of here? What's this fear rooted in? One question I love to use is, "What's the worst thing that could happen?" Don't let the "unknown" scenario live forebodingly in the shadows; pull it out and examine it. Chances are, it's not as bad out in the open as it is when it's hiding. What is the worst that could happen? Will your dog die? Will you die? Will you be solely responsible for melting the polar ice caps? Will your significant other, children, friends, or family abandon you? Put fear in its proper f**king place.

Speaking from a place of acute personal awareness, perfectionism is just another form of fear. My earliest memory of this lifelong affliction dates back to kindergarten, where, rather than use an eraser when I made a mistake in my penmanship, I crumpled up the paper and started over. Nobody was happier when word processors became commercially available than I was. So how do I deal with this fear of imperfection all these years later? Well, I do eat some of my own cooking! First, I remind myself that nobody will suffer or die if there's a typo in a proposal, if I use a few too many "uhms" in a keynote, or if I spill coffee on my crisp white shirt just before a client meeting. Second, I remind myself of that aforementioned axiom about perfect being the enemy of great and refuse to ask myself if something's perfect. That's a question begging for bogus judgment and time-and-energy-wasting perseveration. Instead, I ask myself if I'm on-track or off-track. That helps me stay focused, without diving into the quicksand that is perfectionism.

One of my executive coaching clients was afraid to ask for the raise he knew he deserved. We talked about what was at stake if he didn't get the raise, and I asked, "What's the worst thing that could happen if you do ask?" In answering, he discovered that he was scared his manager would say no outright, and accuse him of being self-interested in the face of tough times at the company. But, knowing what he knew about his boss, once that fear was out in the light, he recognized it for the false story (ahem, assumption!) that it was. He ended up going into the meeting with a much different mindset and got most of what he wanted.

DEALING WITH OUR FEARS

The point of recognizing your fears is to shut them down. Take their power away by asking those questions. Fears are night creatures; shine a light on them and they'll scurry back into their holes. The more you do that, the more confident you'll be. The more confident you are, the more risks you take, the more successful you become, which makes you even more confident, and then? You'll be in the middle of a delightfully healthy cycle.

Make friends with fear. Realize that sometimes when you sense fear, it's legitimate and you'll want to pay attention to it. Many times, though, it's just your own inner critic being an asshole. You'll be able to tell the difference if you have a strong grasp on your values and your purpose.

#NOREGRETS: MORE CONTEXT

As a famous quote by motivational speaker Les Brown points to, most regrets we have are tied to fear: "Too many of us are not living our dreams because we are living our fears."

Fear holds us back, and often when we look back, we wish we would have acted differently. We were too scared to change jobs, ask that person out on a date, make that investment, or go on that trip. These are the things we regret as we get older, but by then it may be too late.

When I was in a job that made me unhappy—in retrospect, I know that it crushed my values of challenge and independence—I quit. Not only did I quit, but I also traveled around the world for a year. And trust me, I unequivocally had fear around that resignation; I absolutely had fear around traveling the world solo; I undeniably had fear around what I was going to do for work once I got back! There was a shit ton of fear. But instead of succumbing to it, I ordered fear to strap in—because it was coming along for the ride.

If I had said no, if I had stayed home, I'd be living with huge regret. I would have missed countless opportunities. I never would have met my husband on the New Zealand leg of my world tour!

THE IMPORTANCE OF SELF-CARE

One aspect of having your shit together that's easy to miss is self-care. Even if you get your values lined up, your purpose perfectly manicured, and your fears smashed to bits, you'll never be able to become a sustained better boss if you don't care for your health. The human body is a machine; it needs maintenance. It needs to be oiled, it needs rest, it needs proper fuel. A lot of very ambitious, successful people end up sacrificing their own health to get ahead, which is not prudent for long-term success. Is it really going to matter that you're making six or seven or eight figures if you drop dead of a preventable heart attack or an untreated gastrointestinal disease leaves you sporting a permanent colostomy bag? This may sound melodramatic, but sadly, I've seen firsthand too many times when these and other health calamities have befallen colleagues who didn't take care of themselves.

Self-care also involves stress management. Stress has a major impact on not only our spirit and emotions, but also on our bodies. Study after study reveals that stress lives in the body in the form of pain, injury, and chronic disease. Better bosses figure out ways to manage their stress and address self-care. That doesn't necessarily mean working two days a week or having daily massage; it simply means they prioritize whatever is needed to maintain their health and wellness. Prioritize eating a certain way, spending time with family, taking a morning run, or honoring the values that aren't always tied to work.

If you're taking care of yourself, not only will you be able to manage your own duties with more success, but you'll also set an amazing example for your team. More people will be inclined to take care of themselves if the boss sets the example.

A pervasive concern I hear voiced by my executive coaching clients who struggle with self-care, from middle managers all the way up to the C-suite, is dissatisfaction with the amount of time they're spending on the most important and strategic matters. Why? Mainly because their minds are buzzing with action items and cluttered with trivia, and that state of internal disruption is compounded by non-stop external interruptions and distractions. To compensate, they work harder and longer hours, and thus the self-care dilemma compounds. I have a few tricks up my sleeve to attack these challenges:

1. **Stop occupying brain space with minutiae.** Most of us exist in a constant state of information overload. Stimuli rush at us constantly from all directions: emails, phone calls, texts, meetings, social media, notifications from our fitness tracking apps, requests from colleagues...and even the thoughts swirling around in our own brains. What happens when we use our minds to remember things? We lose sleep, we forget, we get stressed, we drop the ball, we miss meetings, we pretend to listen. The mind is simply not an effective place to keep track of anything, and inevitably, those thoughts will always upload back to our consciousness at the most inconvenient moments, such as bedtime or, even worse, at 3 a.m.

    Instead, take a few moments on a regular basis to transfer all the commitments and to-dos roaming around your head onto a master list, such as Outlook Tasks, Omnifocus, Asana, or a cloud-based app of your choice. Once you've committed them to a central and safe place, your mind can let go, freeing it up to focus on higher-priority projects or strategic thought.

2. **Meditate.** Yes, you left-brained corporate denizens, I said *meditate*. Please don't roll your eyes or make patchouli oil jokes; rather, please keep reading as a fellow left-brainer explains. You don't need to sit under a tree meditating along the banks of the Ganges River in India, twist yourself into a pretzel, or rush out to buy the latest Lululemon gear to meditate. Yes, meditation is associated with yoga, but *yoga is merely about quieting the over-activity in our heads*. New Age connotations are largely Western creations, not innate or mandatory aspects of yoga and meditation.

In fact, simply put by the 1,800-year-old Yoga Sutras, "Yoga is a method to quiet the fluctuations of the mind." If I can free my mind of the dozens of other things going through it, and give my sole focus to one complex problem or issue while sitting in my ergonomic Herman Miller office chair beneath florescent lights, then that is a huge yogic victory. Some of my most creative ideas and solutions to previously confounding work-related challenges have occurred to me when I hit the pause button on the craziness to relax, even just for a few minutes, in a meditative state.

Just a variation on relaxation, meditation is grounded in physiology. The autonomic nervous system of the human body is divided into the sympathetic system, which is often identified with "fight-or-flight," and the parasympathetic, which triggers "rest and digest." The sense of relaxed control achieved through meditation turns off the fight-or-flight system, allowing the rest and digest response to kick in. Your body registers this with a slower heartbeat, decreased respiration and blood pressure, and return of normal blood flow to that vital organ of thought...your brain. And guess what? That blood flow and reinvigoration goes to the right *and* left sides of your brain.

3. **Get better at saying "No."** Ambitious, successful people tend to overcommit. But due to the finite nature of time, when you say "Yes" to someone or something else, by definition you're saying "No" to something on your own project list. Saying "No" is not about being uncooperative or stingy with your time; rather, it's a self-care tool full of focus and prioritization

   Does this vicious cycle sound familiar? You take on everything that comes your way, you fall further behind, your anxiety level rises, and you constantly burn the candle at both ends—none of which are healthy or sustainable. Steve Jobs put it practically, "Innovation comes from saying no to 1,000 things to make sure we don't get on the wrong track or try to do too much...it's only by saying no that you can concentrate on the things that are really important."

   If you find yourself saying "Yes" to all requests or defaulting to low-impact items on your to-do list, pause to ask yourself, "How does this [meeting, task, project, lunch invitation, board position, volunteer committee post, etc.] support one of my biggest professional and/or personal goals?" If the answer is, "Huh, it doesn't," then question whether you should be saying "Yes" to it.

You'll almost certainly regret the ways you don't take care of yourself. You'll regret letting the dentist appointment lapse for so long that you end up needing a root canal. You'll regret never playing tennis again after college. You'll regret not seeing your elderly grandparents because you were working too much. We all regret these sorts of things. Putting some focus on self-care, whatever that looks like for us individually, helps us live and lead with fewer or #NoRegrets.

LIFE-WORK INFUSION®

You're probably thinking this is all about "work-life balance." Sorry, but no. Work-life balance is probably the most overused bullshit phrase out there. There's no such thing as balance between your work-life and your life-life, especially for people who are ambitious! We don't want balance, and they can't possibly ever be equal. We're not going to have ten hours of playtime for every ten hours a day of work. That's the kind of "balance" the obsolete catchphrase seems to imply. But it's a blatantly unrealistic objective when you really look at it. If you're a goal-oriented person, to always be striving for a goal that isn't ever attainable can be really f**king frustrating.

So I came up with a different way to frame it.

I'm a foodie, and one day it became all the rage to infuse things—as you likely noticed, too. Teas were suddenly infused with acai berry and other trendy anti-oxidants, coffees were infused with Tahitian vanilla and pumpkin spice, and chocolates were infused with exotic spices (thank you to my dear friend Katrina Markoff of Vosges Haut-Chocolat for initiating this personal favorite infusion trend!). I even have an olive oil in my cabinet that's infused with rosemary. It's delicious.

The idea behind infusing our foods and beverages with these elements is to make them taste better, while also making them healthier. A lot of the infused ingredients are superfoods, which pack a lot of flavor and health benefits into small amounts.

That's what we need in our life! We need to infuse what's already there with small elements that will make everything more delicious, healthy, and fulfilling. How can we add more activities into our lives that fill us up and replace the things that drain us? That's the concept behind Life-Work Infusion®.

For me, yoga is part of self-care. There are meditative (see above!) as well as physical benefits to yoga: it helps with strength, flexibility, and agility, and it's a well-documented stress reliever. I try to infuse every week with at least two yoga classes. I'm not doing an equal amount of yoga as work—it's only two classes. It's an infusion—a flavor sprinkled throughout my week—that adds joy and promotes health and stress reduction.

Just as with food and beverages, different tastes appeal to different people, and our palates evolve over time. Everyone gets to define what Life-Work Infusion looks like for them at any given time in life.

One of my clients has a major job at a prominent financial institution. An infusion mechanism we devised for her was working from home two Fridays per month, which allowed her to pick her kids up at school occasionally. It wasn't realistic for her to drive them home from school every day of every week, but she wanted to at least be able to do it sometimes. Being able to pick the kiddos up a couple of times a month lets her lead with fewer regrets. Now she doesn't have to feel remorseful for never being able to await her children at the end of their school day, because her life is infused with that ingredient.

Interestingly, she gets more done on the days she works from home. It's a win-win for her and her employer.

WE ALL NEED A (SELF)-MANAGER

When you're more in touch with your values, understand where your fear is coming from, and identify how to take care of yourself, you're well on your way to having your shit together. And you'll be able to promptly recognize when you're out of alignment. When that happens, you have to self-manage.

The first step in self-management is just noticing, and then taking a moment to figure out an alternative. How do you get back to honoring your values? How do you grapple with the fear? How do you take care of yourself in a small way even though you think you don't have time? How do you show up in any situation at your best when you might be stressed out, tired, irritable, or operating in chaos?

I devised a tool to use with clients called the "Bottle of Your Best-Self." Again, I'll ask a succession of questions such as: "What does the best version of you look like?", "What was a banner day for you in the past, when you were so on your game that you'd like to bottle it up and keep it forever?", "What experiences bring out the best in you?" Now, name that best-version-of-yourself. Give it an identity, or a personal brand if you will. For example, the most alive I've ever felt was skydiving from fifteen thousand feet, so that's "Parachute-Shani." The one thing that never fails to calm me down when I'm stressed out is cuddling with my cats Elaine and Kramer, so I call that magical elixir "Seinfeld-Shani."

Using this tool, I am able to bring a figurative six-pack of Parachute-Shani and/or Seinfeld-Shani to situations when I might be fearful, triggered, or upset. I may only need a sprinkle, or I may need to tap a whole f**king keg of it to recover back to my best self. Do this exercise for yourself, and pop open a bottle of your best-self the next time someone conjures up a painful memory, cuts you off in traffic, or asks you to present impromptu in front of an audience.

BUILDING HABITS

How do we, despite such frequent triggers, continue to show up in a way that makes us proud and honors our values? The answer is in our habits. According to the dictionary, a habit is "An acquired behavior pattern regularly followed until it becomes almost involuntary." If self-managing is something you're not used to doing, don't worry. Like anything else, it just takes practice. You wouldn't expect to compete in a bodybuilding competition because you went to the gym once, right? It's going to take consistent dedication on lots of different machines and lots of different muscles to compete effectively.

It's no different if we've got a goal that isn't so physically obvious. We need the repetition from frequent practice.

The good news is, after some time, it will become involuntary because our brain will start to cooperate. Remember, "If it fires, it wires." If there's a neural pathway in your brain that fires, it can be wired to form new habits or rewired to override the old ones.

This chapter is rife with ideas for aspirational new habits. Perhaps you want to practice:

› Honoring a value you are neglecting at this point in your life
› Noticing your unique filters as you're interacting with other people and making decisions
› Shutting down your fears and inner critics
› Organizing all your to-dos into one central e-location
› Turning off your devices at least an hour before bed to ensure a peaceful night's sleep
› Meditating for fifteen minutes twice a week

> Saying "No" more often to optional commitments that don't help you achieve your goals
> Infusing your weeks with just a little more of something you enjoy doing with friends or family, or even a stretch project at work
> Pouring on the contents of a Bottle of Your Best-Self when you encounter a trigger

One of my favorite quotes of all time is from motivational speaker Zig Ziglar, and it underscores the importance of consistently practicing any new habit or behavior: "People often say that motivation doesn't last. Well, neither does bathing, that's why we recommend it daily." Pick an idea from this list and then practice it daily.

THE FOUR AGREEMENTS

If you're not sure where to begin with the brain wiring, "The Four Agreements" are a great starting point. These agreements come from the book by the same name, by Don Miguel Ruiz:

1. Be impeccable with your word.
2. Don't take things personally.
3. Don't make assumptions.
4. Always do your best.

If everyone on the planet lived by these four simple covenants, imagine how great the world would be.

Even if you don't feel ready to examine your own triggers or do the values work, experiment with living by these easy-to-remember sanity savers. If you find yourself getting upset at a situation, before you react, pause and think, "Am I making an assumption here? Oh yes, I am. Am I taking things personally here? Damn it, yes I am. Okay. I recognize that." Now, instead of reacting, you can respond calmly. Maybe you can even respond with a question instead of an outburst. It's a great first step towards healthy self-management.

THAT'S NOT HARD

On one of my favorite websites, Whole30.com, there are numerous suggestions to help participants get through their dietary cleanse. One of their philosophies has really impacted me and applies to a lot of what we're doing here.

Part of the Whole30 program is to cut dairy for a month. At first glance, that sounded impossible to me: no cheese, no butter, no ice cream, not even any creamer for my coffee? Does anyone have the Devil's cell number? I'd rather sell my soul than give up brie. FML, that's hard!

Except that it really isn't. In one of their pep talks they state, "Don't you dare tell us this is hard. Quitting heroin is hard. Beating cancer is hard. Drinking your coffee black. Is. Not. Hard."

That was a powerful perspective shift for me, as someone who really likes milk in her coffee. I think about this statement anytime I'm trying to do something I know is good for me but, nevertheless, am resisting because I think, "It's hard." I remind myself, "Drinking coffee black is not hard! And this is not hard either."

Bottom line—do what you need to do to get your own shit together! As speaker and author Abraham Hicks said, "You cannot get sick enough to help sick people get better. You cannot get poor enough to help poor people thrive. It is only in your thriving that you have anything to offer anyone. If you're wanting to be of an advantage to others, be as tapped in, tuned in, turned on as you can possibly be."

Better Boss Baby Steps:

Work Continuously on
Having My Own Shit Together:

› Classify your top five values, the ones that truly make you tick. Use the questions in this chapter or another framework.

› Catch yourself when making assumptions and ponder what circumstances or personal filters led to them.

› Pinpoint your primary reaction to fear along with a support tool to respond more creatively the next time fear surfaces.

› Select one way you can take better care of yourself and find an accountability partner to help you stick to it.

› Download a user-friendly meditation app such as 10% Happier or Headspace to give meditation a try.

› Identify what's in the "Bottle of Your Best Self" and sprinkle it on like cologne when needed.

› Read *The Four Agreements.*

TWO

[As a Better Boss, I commit to:]

TAKE RESPONSIBILITY

TWO

[As a Better Boss, I commit to:]

TAKE RESPONSIBILITY

"Control your own destiny or someone else will."
– Jack Welch

IT'S TIME FOR A TOUGH TRUTH: Everything in your life is your responsibility. You're responsible for your own decisions; you're responsible for the quality of your relationships; and you're responsible for your own growth and development.

In a business development role I had some years ago, I was waiting for the head of marketing to respond to a question I'd posed to her via email before I could follow up with a prospect, when one of my colleagues asked me about it.

"Have you made any progress on this?" she asked.

"No," I griped. "I'm really frustrated. I've been waiting for input from Priya in marketing. I've emailed her a couple of times now, and she just isn't getting back to me!"

My colleague looked at me thoughtfully and said without missing a beat, "That's bullshit." I was floored for a second. "That shouldn't stop you," she went on. "It's always up to you."

It was that last sentence that caught me. It's always up to you. The truth was, waiting on marketing was just an excuse. There was no reason I couldn't move the sales process forward without her.

It's always up to you. When you have the guts to own this, to really believe that it is always up to you, you become more engaged in your own life. You stop blaming and pointing fingers. You stop focusing on obstacles and start focusing on solutions. How can you move things forward anyway?

It's always up to you. If you don't believe this, you can slip way too easily into the victim mentality. Great leaders never want to be perceived as victims; that's why, so often, they don't ask for help. But that's a fallacy about leadership and victimhood—asking for help doesn't make you weak or needy; it's the attitude you have that does. If you take responsibility, if you realize that it's always up to you, then you can also assess the situation, evaluate your own limits, and know with confidence when you legitimately need help. No one can do everything; knowing what you can and can't do, and asking for help to make up the difference, is part of taking responsibility and being a true leader.

In contrast, victims don't ask for help because they know their limits. Rather, victims ask for help because they cling to a "poor me" attitude, are needy, want attention, and/or sadly have given up before even trying. That's 180-degrees opposite of what a better boss would do.

It's not the asking; it's the attitude. *Better bosses ask for help with a vision instead of a complaint.*

THE CIRCLES OF INFLUENCE AND CONTROL

Imagine three concentric circles—one inside another, inside another. The smallest circle inside is the only part of our life that we're actually in control of—ourselves. It's our thoughts, feelings, emotions, and actions. That's why it's the smallest circle.

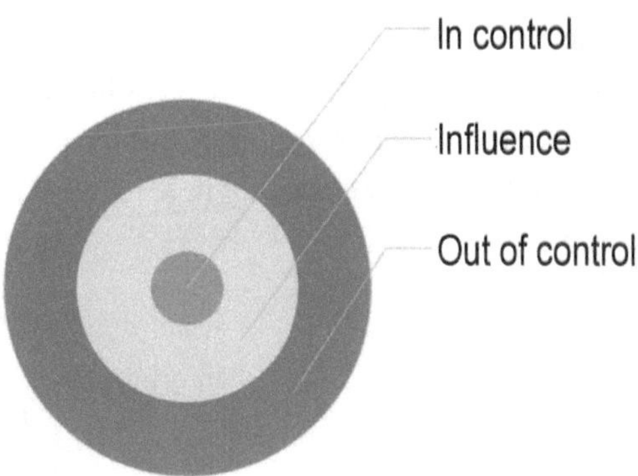

The outermost part of the three circles represents everything that seems out of our control, such as traffic, bad weather, flight delays, new leadership at our company or in our country, noisy open office environments, or supply chain delays. It's the economy; it's a store running out of our favorite product; it's office politics, relentless competitors, or unresponsive colleagues. (Do I sound like new lyrics for the Alanis Morissette song "Ironic" yet?) There are so many things outside of our control—the list is endless. And yet, these are the things we spend so much time obsessing about. What a waste of time!

The second circle, the middle band of the three, is the Circle of Influence. This is where the magic is. A lot of people mistakenly believe this sphere of influence holds matters which are also outside of their control, so they retreat into their small, center circle. That's what they know, and that's where they feel safe. They hide. It's a response of fear, one that ignores the possibilities of the Circle of Influence. There are ways to make that middle band wider, rather than narrower, but we won't see how if we're hiding in the center.

Getting our own shit together is how we affect the inner circle: it's learning to control our own emotions and fears, and showing up the way we want to show up. When we get that under control, then we can play more successfully in the Circle of Influence. That circle is where we might not have *control*, but we do have *influence*—i.e. the place where it's always up to you! Don't overlook it.

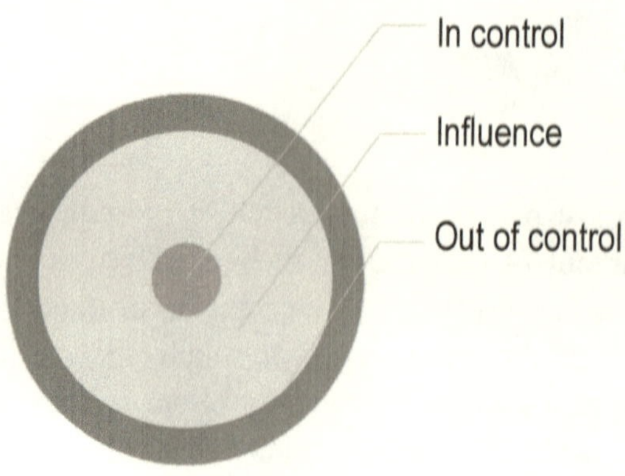

I thought I couldn't make that sales call because I was waiting on marketing. I thought it was out of my control. But in fact, that wasn't entirely true. I could exert my own influence to make the sales call happen anyway. We discussed a similar example during a workshop I taught recently to a group of senior B2B media salespeople who are often stonewalled by clients with the "no budget" excuse. Instead of letting discouragement get the best of us in those circumstances, we talked about ways to influence that included helping their marketing contacts advocate upstream to the CFO (or even CEO, as Salesforce founder Marc Benioff has pointed to as one of their keys to success). In other words, present business-savvy solutions that directly support the organization's strategic and/or financial objectives and have a clear-cut ROI. There's rarely budget that can't be found or reallocated when the right business case exists.

Increasing the width of that middle circle, exercising our influence when we don't necessarily have control, means being creative. It means being proactive, and not reactive, to our situation.

Part of this is realizing that we have choices. We can choose to continue to behave as though these things are out of our control, or we can choose to influence. There will always be external obstacles and internal, perceived obstacles, but we can still choose which path we want to take. Are we going to choose to let fear hold us back, or are we going to choose to put a leash on fear and drag it along with us? Are we going to allow ourselves to be triggered? Or are we going to pause, question whether we're making assumptions or taking things personally, and shift perspectives as necessary to ensure success? Are we going to take a dismissive "No" for an answer when we have a win-win solution for a client, or will we choose to influence other decision makers with confidence and smart business acumen?

We must live with the choices we make; let's not be so timid that we forget we have them. As an anonymous adage teaches us, "Pain is inevitable, but suffering is optional."

RESPONDING AS A LEADER

If you're a leader in an organization, and you don't feel as if you have the tools you need to succeed, is it really productive to complain about it and/or be complacent and not pursue the tools you need? What can you do to equip yourself? Today, there are endless resources, not the least of which is The Better Boss Project, that you can find for yourself to support your own success.

I am quite familiar with potentially feeling trapped and ill-equipped to execute on one of my responsibilities. As a quick example, when I took the role as COO of that B2B marketing company in Colorado (which included running IT), I knew nothing about enterprise hardware and software, but I surely didn't wait for the Ghost of Christmas Future to hand me an updated technology solution on a silver platter. Instead, I went online and did voluminous research. I networked with people who were knowledgeable in the space. I spoke at length to various vendors. And I made a well-informed decision to migrate the company to the cloud in 2007 when few people had heard of it, and saved the company lots of money and headaches as a result.

More recently, I was co-leading a meeting when a colleague (with whom I actually have a fantastic relationship) said something incredibly negative, in front of a room of twenty-five people! I don't think he realized how dispiriting his comment was, but it landed very painfully for me. I was in front of this small crowd, co-leading a meeting, and his words struck me like a knife and blew me way off course.

In that moment, I initially wanted to snap right back at him, to go on the offensive to protect my hurt feelings. Instead, I decided to wait before responding and process what had happened. I started getting pretty emotional; anger, really, is sometimes just a way to mask a more vulnerable pain, so when I didn't give in to the anger, the real emotion came through. What I actually felt was a little embarrassment, so I asked my co-leader to take over. I took a minute to myself to regroup and shift my energy before re-engaging with the group. The meeting could've turned really ugly at that point. Instead, I remembered to take responsibility and made a different choice. I was proactive, not reactive. And a way more responsible leader during an uncomfortable situation as a result.

GETTING HIRED WITHOUT A PEDIGREE

To further illustrate the take responsibility credo, I want to layer in some additional detail to the story I told in the Introduction about getting hired at Goldman Sachs. As already alluded to, investment banks were not accustomed to looking at resumes with the University of Miami (aka "The U") at the top in the Education section. It was not a school that they commonly recruited from. Usually, their recruits came from Harvard, Yale, Princeton, Wharton—the Ivy Leagues—and maybe Duke, Northwestern, or Berkeley.

But I didn't waiver. I certainly didn't interview with the mindset that they might not accept my school. I never thought to apologize for it, because I was a straight A student at an excellent university. Plus, I had over a year of great experience under my belt from having been through the management training program at Chase Manhattan Bank. And it worked. I had dozens of interviews, but in the end, Goldman hired me.

Even after I was hired, people continued to ask me if I regretted going to The U. Hell no! Why would I? I got a great education and had a ton of fun! Why settle for monotonous on-campus fraternity parties when South Beach and the Florida Keys beckon? Keep those musty, ivy-covered buildings; I'll take Calle Ocho and the Coconut Grove Arts Festival instead. Our football team won the national championship three times in my era. But with so many people asking this question, I couldn't help it—I started to doubt myself. Could I really be as successful as my colleagues without a Yale degree?

Instead of lingering in doubt, I worked my ass off. I had ever-improving technical skills, great communication skills, and high emotional intelligence. Years later, the head of analyst recruiting conducted an analysis of everyone who had gone through Goldman's financial analyst program from its inception in the early 1980s until about 2000. They identified the top twenty-five analysts of all time, and I smiled from ear to ear when I heard I had made that prestigious list. That never would have happened had I allowed fear to stop me. What if I had shut myself down before even applying? What if I had bought into the narrative that one needs an Ivy League education to succeed at an elite firm like Goldman? I took responsibility for my career, chose to do my very best, and succeeded—despite the proverbial perception cards being stacked against me.

HEED THE ORACLE OF KENTUCKY

Taking responsibility as a better boss means having high self-awareness and owning your own success. A modern leader who stands out in this regard is David Novak, former CEO of Yum! Brands, the holding company for Taco Bell, Pizza Hut, and KFC. During David's tenure, Yum! achieved enviably high shareholder returns in a notoriously challenging industry. So what was his secret sauce, so to speak? He was known to be a master of employee recognition and spent much of his time outside the confines of his corner office. In addition, and especially applicable to the theme of taking responsibility, he wasn't afraid to appear imperfect or ask for help! Here are a few specific and easily replicable nuggets from his philosophy:

› **Be self-aware.** Every January, Novak did what he referred to as the "3x5 exercise," in which he described how he saw himself currently—strengths and weaknesses—on the front side of an index card, and on the back side, he listed how he could be even more effective going forward. He didn't stop there. He then distributed a copy of this index card to the top forty people at Yum! and asked for their support ("This is what I'm working on and I'd like your help. Please save me from myself.") and feedback ("Did I miss anything that will help me? I want to do my very best as a leader."). Of course, those forty people also did the 3x5 exercise, cascading this best practice throughout the company.

› **Be proactive with managing your career.** The story Novak told around this was a result of his own self-awareness. Prior to leading Yum!, Novak was president of both KFC and Pizza Hut and held senior management positions at PepsiCo. But that was not an obvious career path for a marketing guy. Upon receiving feedback from then PepsiCo CEO Wayne Calloway that he was a superb marketer but not equipped to be president of a division, Novak proactively pursued intermediate roles that would augment his skill set and allow him to demonstrate that he was capable of running not only a division, but also an entire company.

› **Have a spirit of continuous improvement.** Novak shares my view that even highly successful people can up their game. He coached his direct reports to do what he called the Hotshot Replaces Me exercise. It goes a little something like this: "If you're self-aware and really know your business, then you know what needs to be done but you haven't done it yet. So do it before someone brings in a hotshot to replace you."

David Novak is just a regular guy, and any better boss can emulate his best practices. As such, as we end this chapter, let me leave you with a few questions to ponder:

› How can you take more responsibility for circumstances that, upon first glance, seem out of your control?
› How can you be more creative in your decision making?
› What can you do to improve important relationships?
› What additional skills or experience can you pursue that will enable you to take more control over your own growth, development, career trajectory, and happiness?

Better Boss Baby Steps:

Take Responsibility

> Lead with a vision instead of a complaint next time you need to ask for help.

> Identify one thing you want that you previously deemed out of your control and brainstorm ways you can assert influence to make it happen.

> Choose a shift to a more constructive perspective next time you get upset or face an obstacle.

> Try the 3x5 exercise with a few trusted people.

THREE
[As a Better Boss, I commit to:]

KEEP A "TO-BE" LIST

THREE

[As a Better Boss, I commit to:]

KEEP A "TO-BE" LIST

"When I was 5 years old, my mother always told me that happiness was the key to life. When I went to school, they asked me what I wanted to be when I grew up. I wrote down 'happy.' They told me I didn't understand the assignment, and I told them they didn't understand life."
—John Lennon

ONE OF THE MOST IMPACTFUL things I have learned in my adult life is the difference between being and doing. As someone who is highly driven and extremely action-oriented, I always have been and probably always will be obsessed with my to-do list. I literally get adrenaline surging through my veins when I cross things off it, because I love getting shit done.

The problem is, if you're motoring through life just plowing through your to-dos, chances are you aren't thinking about your mindset. That's when you run the risk of losing your effectiveness, or even ending up a complete personal train wreck. Focusing on how you want to be (i.e. how you want to show up while you're in action) can make all the difference. In other words, it's how you show up as a total package—actions plus intentions, attitude, energy, tone, body language, etc.

Let me illustrate with an example: Marilyn Monroe was walking down a Manhattan street right in the middle of a tightly clustered group of girlfriends. Let's say it was Madison Avenue. They had been walking that way for several blocks, at which point one of the women finally expressed her surprise at the lack of fanfare—that nobody had noticed that the Marilyn Monroe was nearby. Never one to shy away from a challenge, Marilyn said, "Oh yeah, watch this!" She flipped an invisible internal switch and proceeded to glide out a few steps in front of her friends, head up, shoulders back, hips swaying broadly. Suddenly, throngs of bystanders were screaming some variety of, "Look, it's Marilyn Monroe!"

In both cases, Marilyn was technically doing the same thing— walking down the street. In the first instance, her way of being while walking was unassuming and inconspicuous. But in the latter, she was be-ing Marilyn Monroe in all her attention-seeking, sex kitten glory. *Very different ways of being, and thus, very different impact and outcome.*

Similarly, a leader can speak the same words verbatim but have them land differently depending on how they "be"—the tone and spirit in which they're delivered. Meek and tentative versus strong and confident. Trite and insincere versus empathetic and genuine. Annoyed and judgmental versus patient and open-minded. Distracted and disinterested versus attentive and passionate.

While this may seem obvious, I posit that most of us overachieving, goal-setting, type-A personalities who have ascended to leadership roles don't think nearly enough about how we show up while in just-get-it-done, execution mode.

That's why there are some decent managers out there, but not enough true leaders.

In case you're wondering, my intent while do-ing the writing of this book was to be conversational, provocative, funny and sometimes irreverent, serious when called for, and always in service of shaping more better bosses.

TOOLS FOR YOUR BETTER BOSS BELT: YOUR INNER RADIO

So how can you pay more attention to how you're being while you're undertaking all the *doing?* Great question!

I'm going to share a tool I've been using for years to coach clients through challenges and daunting circumstances of all types. It's a tool that helps people call upon and leverage valuable inner resources that lie dormant or are vastly underutilized, like muscles that haven't been flexed in years. It's premised on a radio analogy: people are like radios in that we all have the ability to tune into an endless number of stations—or pieces of ourselves—such as strengths, attitudes, behaviors, thoughts, energies, and emotions. Just as most of us literally have a favorite radio station or two, we figuratively tune into a few characteristic personality and behavioral "stations" either subconsciously because they're deeply ingrained habits, or consciously to remain within our comfort zones.

With today's awesome technology, we can tune into any radio station in the world or even curate our own. Nevertheless, most people have a couple of stations that tend to be their go-tos. You like classic rock, hip hop, 80s music, country, or maybe Elvis, and the stations in that genre are your default. But that doesn't mean you don't have access to other stations, right? They're all available, ready for a shower or carpool karaoke.

The same is true for your way of being.

You have a default mode, which is your typical way of being. But you have a whole host of other options inside of you as well. Human beings are complex and layered, after all, and you are no exception. You've got radio stations inside you that you can tune into any time you want. Why not recognize those? This is a great way to call up new ways of being that are outside your default, like Marilyn Monroe did on Madison Avenue. What is your station for showing up confidently? What's your station for remaining calm? What's your station to raise your energy level? Give them all entertaining names, and tune in when you need them. They're all accessible, and once you name them, they're that much easier to find.

Here's how it works: When a situation calls for it, you mentally select the specific station that can instantly trigger the inner resource(s) you require to succeed. For example:

› **Need to conjure up some extra confidence?** Mentally tune into a station that represents you in particularly confident circumstances. Or perhaps a Don Draper station—that Mad Men character can sell ice to Eskimos.

› **Want to be calmer in some notoriously stressful situation?** Try a Dalai Lama channel. Or maybe the Dos Equis man or Jimmy Buffet resonates more for you.

› **Struggling to make a mission-critical business decision?** Perhaps a Steve Jobs or Sheryl Sandberg station could put you in the right frame of mind. If not, think about it from the perspective of any leader you admire, and then tune in loud and clear.

› **Feeling like an underdog?** Channel your inner Jerry McGuire to stoke confidence and connect with values and aspects of your situation that energize you. Or a time you succeeded against all odds.

› **Distracted?** Create a station that reminds you of how present in every single moment you felt during the blissful weekend you once spent in a remote spot without cell service.

› **Want to be more empathetic in an awkward situation?** Hit the mental button for the station you created to remind you of the inspiring video that went viral last year and brought you and many others to tears.

› **Getting too verbose?** How about a Twitter station so you can say it in 140 characters or less?

› **Overdue for an infusion of your clever sense of humor into an intense conversation?** Seek out the wavelength of Jimmy Kimmel, Melissa McCarthy, Chris Rock, or any personal favorite comedic personality.

These are your tools, so make them as personally relevant and meaningful for you as possible. The suggestions above are just that—suggestions. Here are some questions to assist in thinking through your own inner radio lineup:

› What are some areas in which you typically shine and want to reinforce or strengthen further?

› In what areas do you typically struggle or get stuck?

› What constructive feedback have you received that you want to address going forward?

› What do you typically find yourself wishing you had done more or less of?

> What do you most admire in other people that you want to emulate?
> The answers to such questions will help inform what radio stations would be most supportive for you.

THE TO-BE LIST

I make a to-be list for any meeting I go into, or in advance of important events. For example, if I'm going to facilitate a workshop that's full of millennials, I could do it in a way that would bore them to tears, as if I were talking to their great-grandparents. Or I could do it in a way that would resonate with them. It all depends on the mindset I bring, and how I decide to be. My to-be list for that facilitation might look like something like this:

To Be:
> Fun and engaging
> Casual and informal
> Brief and succinct
> Curious and armed with lots of stimulating questions

Those are ways of being that I think will resonate with millennials. I recommend this type of intentionality behind your to-be list to lock in your success.

A doing/being analogy I use frequently I learned from Abraham Hicks. Imagine that you want to toast some bread—you take the bread out of the refrigerator, you undo the twist-tie on the bag, you take two pieces of bread out. Then, you put them in the toaster and press the toast button. While you're waiting, you grab a plate from the cabinet and a knife from the drawer and pull out jam from the fridge. But did you check to make sure the toaster is plugged in? If there's no electrical connection, you're going to work really hard to make that toast, to no avail. Sure, the bread will eventually warm up and reach room temperature, but it won't be toasted.

The to-be list is like plugging in the toaster. The toaster cord gives you the literal connection to make it easy; figuratively, it's about connecting to who you need to be for success.

Ok, now that you have a good understanding of the difference between doing and being, let's take it a step further. The way many people approach life is with the *Have→Do→Be* mentality: "If I could just have the sum of money I want, I could do all the shopping and travel I want, and then I will be happy." But that only sets up a victim mentality or a frustratingly elusive quest for happiness.

What about the reverse? What if our mentality were *Be→Do→Have?* "If I can be happy (and whatever other relevant ways of being you choose) while I'm doing my job (i.e. interacting with customers/colleagues/ vendors/stakeholders/friends/family/ neighbors), I stand a much higher chance of success and will have the financial abundance to shop and travel as I wish to." It's flipping around the way we naturally think. Many of us think, "If I just have this, if I just have that, I'll be happy." But it doesn't work that way. Another quotable truism from Dan Harris's book *10% Happier* fits like a glove here: "We live so much of our lives pushed forward by these 'if only' thoughts, and yet the itch remains. The pursuit of happiness becomes the source of our unhappiness."

Bottom line, be happy first.

To be clear, I am not suggesting that the doing doesn't matter! To the contrary. A great read on this very topic is *Simple Happy* by Andy Feld. In a nutshell, he shares that for a long time, he thought the way to accomplish whatever you want in life was to (1) set the goal, (2) create the plan, and (3) take specific action. Then he realized he was missing a final crucial step: (4) be an emotional match to what you want. In other words, line up what you're doing with the ways of being that will most effectively propel you towards success.

THE BETTER BOSS MINDSET

The *Be→Do→Have* mentality is the mindset needed to truly be a better boss. It's infinitely more motivating to lead this way; the framework from which you lead is simply more inspiring. Let's take another example, because this is a radical shift.

"If we could just have that new product finished, then we could do all the selling we need to, and then we would be successful." That's victim headspace, the *Have→Do→Be*.

Why not say this instead: "If we are being innovative, open-minded, and collaborative while we're doing our product development, then we will have the new product that our clients crave." *Be→Do→Have*! The difference there, as organizational development guru Larry Wilson famously described, is playing to win, rather than playing not to lose.

Learn to distinguish which way of being to bring into any given situation. Is my way of being going to help me win, or is this a way to merely avoid losing? One attitude is all confidence, grounded in your skill. Playing not to lose, on the other hand, comes inherently from a place of fear. Let's examine a couple of prominent examples, one from sports and one from business.

In the 2016 Super Bowl, Peyton Manning and the Denver Broncos were playing to win. It was Manning's last year in the NFL, and he wanted one more ring. He knew the odds were against him, but he was playing for his legacy and to leave a championship mark on the Denver Broncos.

Cam Newton and the Carolina Panthers were seemingly playing not to lose, even though they were favored to win. Indications from Las Vegas bookmakers showed 70 to 80 percent of the public wagering was on Carolina. Yet they lost, and Denver and Peyton Manning took home that ring.

When Samsung released the Galaxy Note 7 in 2016, they were playing not to lose. They didn't want to lose to Apple, so they rushed to sell this phone before it was ready. As a result, they ended up executing a massive recall after the phones started exploding in consumers' hands.

Apple has been playing to win for a long time. They launched the whole touch-screen smartphone category. Not all their innovations are home runs like the iPod and iPhone, but they never stop playing to win. In contrast, other smartphone manufacturers have rushed to follow Apple's lead in order not to lose.

These examples illustrate that *organizations have ways of being and doing* just like individuals do, and different ways of being while doing lead to very different outcomes. It's up to better bosses to model and encourage productive ways of being for themselves, their team, and the entire organization.

Better Boss Baby Steps:

Keep a "To-Be" List

› Name and program at least 3 "Be-ing" stations on your "Inner Radio."

› Make a "To Be" list in advance of your next important meeting or conversation.

› Redesign something you've previously looked at as "*Have→Do→Be*" into a "*Be→Do→Have*" framework and notice what changes.

› Contemplate an aspect of your life where you want to change from "playing not to lose" to "playing to win" and adjust accordingly.

FOUR

ENGAGE PEOPLE BY HAVING ACTUAL CONVERSATIONS

FOUR

[As a Better Boss, I commit to:]

ENGAGE PEOPLE BY HAVING ACTUAL CONVERSATIONS

"God gave us two ears and one mouth, so we ought to listen twice as much as we speak."
– Irish Proverb

WE ALL RECOGNIZE HOW IMPORTANT trust is in the workplace, but building it is easier said than done. How do you get people to trust you when it's not a switch you can just flip? You certainly can't say to your staff, "Trust me," and have them automatically comply. There are certain things you can mandate to your people, but trust isn't one of them. It's developed over time.

You've got to actually have a relationship with people to truly trust them and to have them trust you. Relationships are built on communication, and the right kind of conversations build trust. If leaders are using conversation only to tell people what to do, they are not engendering trust.

My personal worst bad-boss nightmare involved an unbelievable comment he made on an all-staff call after the third woman announced she was pregnant in a very short period of time. I shit you not, he actually said, "Okay, I'm announcing a new tubal ligation policy." He thought he was being funny, but it was offensive, and I received a barrage of complaints immediately—from men and women alike. Among many roles, I oversaw HR, and there was nobody to whom I could escalate other than the offender himself. I knew it wouldn't go well, but I felt I had an ethical obligation to bring it to his attention. Rather than hearing me out, trying to understand what line he had crossed, and realizing he had some proverbial broken glass to clean up, he went ape-shit and demanded to know specifically who had lodged complaints. I told him it was confidential, so he threatened to fire me. Stuck between the rock placed by this asshole and a hard place, I decided to go back to every person who had lodged a complaint, fill each of them in on the situation, and ask permission to identify them in his witch hunt. Strength in numbers, we figured. I also briefed an HR attorney in case things got utterly out of hand. It was messy and demoralizing for all of us. Sadly, it was not the first or last time he did or said something I'd define as bad-boss behavior, which repelled rather than generated trust.

MAINTAIN CLEAN A.I.R.

So why aren't impactful, trust-building conversations happening in the workplace (or at home, quite frankly) more regularly?

› Technology has turned many people into automatons who use email, text, and social media as a replacement for authentic, thoughtful communication.

> Most managers are uncomfortable with, and/or ineffective at having conversations that fall outside the realm of triviality and/or praise.
> It's not rewarded and/or modeled by enough senior leaders, and thus does not pervade the culture.

Those are some formidable, yet not insurmountable, barriers. This chapter and parts of many others contain tips and tricks for scaling such walls. Let's start with a general rule of thumb: when communicating, better bosses maintain "clean A.I.R.", which stands for Authenticity, Integrity, and Respect. When your communication features those qualities, you build trust. Think about the best leaders you've known. I'll wager their "ways of being" when they communicate are genuine, candid, and gracious—another way to describe clean A.I.R.

THE COACHING CONVERSATION

The most important conversation you can learn to have as a better boss is a coaching conversation. When you're asking more questions and giving fewer instructions, that's essentially coaching. I'll showcase a simple and repeatable coaching framework later in this chapter.

A better boss, i.e. someone who has coaching conversations, is a boss who sets very clear goals and expectations other people can rally around. They help people learn to solve their own problems. They delegate with confidence, because their people are much more likely to follow up and be accountable. Productivity, engagement, and loyalty will all increase. When those kinds of relationships exist within a team, it becomes easier to have more difficult conversations, too. Remember, not every conversation, even with your highest performers, is going to be an easy one. That's one of the main reasons why, for a better boss, building trust and communicating with clean A.I.R is so vital.

A coach, in any context, is there to propel people to become better at what they're already interested in doing. They're not necessarily better at the "sport" than the person they're coaching. A good coach:

› Helps people tap into their vision and create action toward realizing their goals.
› Brings out the best in others, seeing things performers don't necessarily perceive on their own. They provide actionable feedback and push people harder than they push themselves.
› Helps people process events in their lives, shift perspectives, and adopt constructive mindsets for action.
› Supports accountability in ways that the coachee wants to be held accountable. It shouldn't feel forced.

Coaching is about asking curious and open-ended questions that encourage a thoughtful response. You're not looking for just a single-word answer, and you're not asking a leading question, hoping for a specific response. This means letting go of those pesky judgments and assumptions and earnestly questioning to learn what's really going on.

Harking back to earlier chapters, what assumptions can you let go of? What assumptions do you make about employees who come from other countries? What assumptions do you hold about people who come from outside your industry versus those from inside your industry? What assumptions do you make about people who work from home versus those who work in the office? Those assumptions and judgments cut off trust-building communication before it can even begin.

As a boss, you can't possibly be better at everyone's job than they are. You don't have the time, and you're not as close to it. Let the people who are immersed in their jobs every day be involved in solving problems, innovating, and creating continuous improvement. Don't just dictate that stuff. Involve them, and trust them.

THE THREE LEVELS OF LISTENING

An essential part of being a good coach is being a good listener. A lot of people *think* they're good listeners, but they're painfully wrong. If you're truly a good listener, you are listening intently at three different levels.

The first level is "self-focused" listening. Sadly, this is the extent of most people's listening skills. If you limit your listening to level one, you're only hearing parts of what someone says because you're most likely thinking about what you want to say next. You're already planning how you're going to refute what was said or how you can sound smart. Or maybe you're thinking about what you want for lunch. Regardless of what thoughts are swirling around in your brain, you're more focused on yourself than on whoever is talking to you.

Level two listening is "other-person" focused. Here, you're actually listening to the other person. You are attentive to and processing what that person is saying, doing a downright good job of tuning out your own thoughts and distractions.

At the third level of listening, "all-focused", you're able to listen to more than just words. You're listening for what's underneath the facts and information contained in the words themselves, such as values, feelings, and beliefs. At this level, you're also listening more holistically to everything that's going on in the surroundings. It could be body language, tone of voice, facial expressions, and energy level. It's not only such non-verbals, but also other signals in the environment in which you're having the conversation. Noticing a messy office or an OCD-level of orderliness is a part of listening at level three, just as much as discerning great eye contact or a case of the sniffles.

Better bosses listen at all three levels. They keenly focus on the other person, respond organically, stay curious, and notice all sorts of cues and clues in the full space.

PICK UP THE PHONE

I've yet to find anyone who has mastered the art of accurately "listening" via email. In fact, many of us avoid conversation entirely, by defaulting to email. Don't get me wrong. I'm a huge fan of devices and software in a variety of contexts—as long as they improve productivity, enhance collaboration, and/or save time. Here's the thing about email: the way most people utilize it does not fit any of those criteria. Let me illustrate with a few stereotypical scenarios I see when coaching people through professional communication challenges, along with some tips for mitigating them.

› **The email novelette.** When you send painfully long emails, what are the odds the recipient(s) read it, took the requested action, or replied? Pretty slim. The ramification is that you'll then spend additional time following up, maybe resending the same ineffective email (which won't get read the second or third time, either). And perhaps you've killed your productivity further, insomuch as the lack of reply created a bottleneck to your moving forward on a project or following up with a customer.

> #hint: If an email needs to be more than a few short paragraphs, pick up the phone instead. You can then follow up with a much shorter email to share files or other information they'll need.

› **The email Ping-Pong game.** You know the ones I'm referring to, with trivial threads back and forth ad nauseam. Research shows that interruptions cost people between three and fifteen minutes in lost productivity. With the hundreds of emails we're already getting each day, why clutter the inbox with a litany of emails that string along a subject that could have been nailed in one short and sweet phone call?

> #hint: If the subject line starts to look like this: "Re:Re:Re:Re:Re:Re:," please pick up the phone and end the time-consuming volley.

› **The email drama.** Let's take this example: "I can't believe this!!!!" Based on that emailed statement, am I excited? Angry? Surprised? Or just punctuation happy? That's right—you don't really know, do you? Email lacks the non-verbal cues, tone of voice clues, and other nuances that show up in actual conversation. Yet, in the absence of knowing true feelings, recipients often interpret the sender's intention in a way that causes them to waste time, such as pouting or overanalyzing, or with actions such as responding with a long, defensive email, or worse yet, involving other people in unnecessary gossip or game theorizing.

#hint: If an email topic is potentially sensitive or open to misinterpretation, pick up the phone and save the soap opera for Netflix.

TOOLS FOR YOUR BETTER BOSS BELT: THE DISCUSS™ MODEL

"I suppose it is tempting, if the only tool you have is a hammer, to treat everything as if it were a nail," explains the well-known adage by psychologist Abraham Maslow. At last, it's time to learn an alternative conversation tool to utilize instead of merely relying on the highly directive, command-and-control hammer variety. The DISCUSS™ model is a way to remember how important open-ended conversations are. Even if you can't remember the acronym, the name itself can remind you how you need to engage.

D **stands for Desired Outcome**. That's helping someone set a goal. What does success look like for them?

I **stands for Implication**. Of achieving or not achieving this goal. What are the rewards for success or consequences of not achieving? This piece can help motivate or re-prioritize.

S **stands for Status**. What's the current status of the project, relationship, or situation?

C **stands for Choices.** What choices do I have to move forward? What can I fix or change? What ideas do I have to address this? It's essentially a big brainstorming session. Challenge your coachee in the spirit of the old Chinese proverb, "When the winds of change blow, some people build walls and others build windmills." What are the windmills in this situation?

U **stands for Unify.** Now that you have a long list of choices, it's time to pick! Unify, as coach and coachee, or as better boss and better employee, on which choice or set of choices you want to move forward with.

S **stands for Steps.** What are the action steps that need to be taken next?

S **stands for Schedule**. What's the schedule or timeline for these action steps?

It's a simple model, but it helps structure a multifaceted conversation and keep it on track. It doesn't have to take long; you can get through DISCUSS in as little as four or five minutes if you're focused. It doesn't have to be formal, either. Of course, if your topic is complicated or complex enough, you probably should sit down behind closed doors with notepads or a white board. You can also coach people in the moment, sitting in the back of an Uber or waiting for an elevator.

WHO ARE THE LINDSEY VONNS OF YOUR ORGANIZATION?

Because I lived in Vail, Colorado for a long time, I always root for local skiing superstar, Olympic gold medalist, and World Cup champion, Lindsey Vonn. Imagine if she had neither been told by her parents and coaches early on that she had such potential nor had a path cleared for her to excel. Imagine Vonn had been left in the dark about the rationale for her home schooling or move from Minnesota to Vail. Absurd, right? Of course, it made sense for her to be fully aware of and aligned with those big goals for her future!

Now let's consider that scenario in the organizational realm. Do you keep the identities of your high potential ("hi-po") employees close to the vest? If so, 1985 called and wants its talent management style back (along with its one-piece ski suit). In today's world, we are deep into the era of transparency and proactive people development, and better bosses communicate to top performers their status as such, and then support them with coaching.

Not coaching top performers is the equivalent of a football coach only coaching the benchwarmers and not the first string. It doesn't make sense! We get far more from coaching our good and great performers than we do from coaching the mediocre or poor performers. Not to say we should give up on them; we need to coach them too, perhaps in a somewhat different way with somewhat different goals. But we certainly shouldn't be coaching them to the exclusion of coaching the rest of our team.

While an argument can always be made that anyone is replaceable, both the quantifiable and intangible costs of turnover are certainly highest for the top performers. So, tell and coach your high potentials...or another company will.

TOOLS FOR YOUR BETTER BOSS BELT: THE GRIP™ MODEL

The GRIP™ model was conceived specifically to help better bosses prepare for the tough talks. Whether you need to "get a GRIP" in advance of a difficult conversation with your direct reports, a colleague, spouse or kids, neighbors, or friends, it doesn't matter; you can use this model. It's really for any conversation that you need to have, but about which you don't feel entirely confident. Maybe you're not sure how you want to say it. Maybe you're not sure how the other person's going to react. Either way, it behooves you to do some preparatory leg work.

> *G* **stands for Gather**. Gather your thoughts, gather the facts, and gather the information you think you might need. You may not need to present all of it, but at least you have it in your back pocket, ready to go. This step prepares you to describe the situation objectively and calmly.

> *R* **stands for Responses**. Think through the various reactions the other person is likely to have, and preparatorily formulate your response to those possibilities. Your responses are often natural opportunities to elevate feedback into feedforward, making it actionable and relevant to future performance. More on that in the next chapter.

I **stands for Interests**. Why is it in their best interest to get on the same page with you? Think through what motivates the other person, so that when you move forward it will be considered a win-win. Remember, too, there's a big difference between intrinsic and extrinsic motivators. It's not like you can offer an extrinsic reward in every conversation, such as, "I'll give you a corner office or a special parking spot if you agree to take on this challenging project." Tapping into intrinsic motivations is typically more feasible for you, and often highly appealing for the other person (ahem, they are often remarkably similar to their core values!). For example, will they be able to master a new skill or utilize an underappreciated one, explore an expanded role, connect to a sense of purpose, or gain more autonomy? Be sure to discuss such factors in a sincere way.

P **stands for Practice**. We practice so many insignificant things in life, and yet we don't often take the time to practice for conversations that can make or break careers or relationships. Practice this conversation before you dive in. Or before they sneak up you and you can't avoid engaging in them reactively instead of proactively. Remember, words spoken can never be retracted.

Better bosses build effective, results-oriented cultures where people trust and respect one another. Such cultures absolutely cannot be developed or sustained without a variety of ongoing conversations. Period. British naval historian C. Northcote Parkinson aptly described the frightening alternative: "The void created by the failure to communicate is soon filled with poison, drivel, and misinterpretation."

Better Boss Baby Steps:

Engage People by
Having Actual Conversations

› Notice at what level of listening you tend to stay in with different people at work and at home.

› Make a phone call next time you know it's preferable to email even if it's less convenient.

› Use the DISCUSS™ Model to coach someone, maybe even yourself.

› "Get a GRIP™" before the next tough talk you need to have.

FIVE

[As a Better Boss, I commit to:]

GIVE FREQUENT BALANCED FEED-BACK AND FEEDFORWARD

FIVE

GIVE FREQUENT, BALANCED FEED-BACK AND FEEDFORWARD

"We don't know who discovered water, but we're pretty sure it wasn't a fish."
– Marshall McLuhan, Canadian professor known for predicting the World Wide Web almost thirty years before it was invented

BETTER BOSSES NEED TO BE excellent at giving frequent, balanced, and timely feedback—and feedforward. Feedback, obviously, is based on something that's happened in the past. It's commentary and discussion that looks backward. Feedforward is taking feedback a step further—to make it actionable and relevant to future performance. Feedback delivered in a vacuum with no connection to future performance is not going to be very useful.

One of the goals of The Better Boss Project is to take the stigma away from feedback. If someone states, "I have some feedback for you," more often than not, our guard goes wayyyy up. We can quickly get defensive, because our culture teaches us to assume feedback is negative. That shouldn't be the case. Too many managers don't give enough positive feedback and reinforcement. Or, if they do, it's completely lame—something like, "Great job." I'm sorry, but that's worthless and lazy. Be specific. Exactly what about it was great? What was the impact the great job had on people? What do you want them to continue doing or do more of?

Better bosses deliver just as much, if not more, positive feedback as they do constructive or negative feedback.

The biggest excuse I hear from managers in terms of why they aren't delivering more frequent feedback and feedforward is that they don't have time. Come on. That's lazy, too! It doesn't take much time to shoot a quick email or IM, or have a 30-second conversation. The other pushback I hear is "I don't know how" or "I don't do it well." Stay tuned—you're about to learn a couple of simple and repeatable tools, so that's no longer a viable excuse.

SIDE NOTE ON NUANCE

Before I introduce the tools, a quick word on nuance. While you can utilize these structures the same way for anyone at any time, be sure to tailor your words to the type of person with whom you're engaging. Everyone receives feedback/forward differently, and obviously, your pace, tone, and word choice will differ with people who are highly sensitive versus those who prefer direct and blunt, for example. Meet people where they are; talk to them in a way that is going to connect with them most effectively.

Part of that is getting to know people as you manage them. There are many great tools and assessments that can help your team learn more about their own and their colleagues' styles, and you'll benefit as their leader in the process.

TOOLS FOR YOUR BETTER BOSS BELT: THE PINOT™ MODEL

The PINOT™ model is a series of best practices for delivering feedback and feedforward. I'm not only a foodie, but also a wine lover. I particularly enjoy Pinot Noir, so it served as inspiration when developing this model.

P **is for Permission.** Simply ask, "Is now a good time?" Don't just bowl someone over with feedback/forward; check in first to see if the other person is free. Maybe he's in a hurry or up against a tight deadline. Maybe she's on the way to a meeting or just had a fight with her spouse. Get permission to give feedback/forward, because in a lot of cases, timing is everything.

I **stands for Interactive**. This means *listen!* Even when you initiate the feedback/forward, take time to listen and ask questions. Feedback/forward should not be one-directional. It's an opportunity to use the coaching skills you learned in the last chapter. Be conscious of any assumptions, ask curious, non-judgmental questions, and listen for the answers.

N **stands for No bullshit.** No BS. This is a reminder to communicate with clean A.I.R. when you're sharing feedback/forward. Be who you are. If people sense you're not being genuine and respectful, they won't take you seriously and/or will dismiss the message. Keeping it neutral is the other important aspect of No BS. It's easier to avoid getting personal or emotional when you limit the feedback to business issues.

O **stands for Often.** Feedback/forward should be given in a continuous and timely matter. I'm not actually comparing your team to dogs, but I think this analogy is pretty sound: Think about training a puppy. If Fido poops in the house and you wait a week to stick his nose in the mess, he's not going to make the cause-effect connection. Feedback/forward offered early and often has a far better chance of sinking in and making an impact.

T **stands for Thanks.** Much like the opening practice of asking permission, remember to thank people for their time and contributions to the feedback/forward discussion.

If you stray from any of these aspects, your feedback/forward won't land. For example, if you neglect the "N" (No BS) and couch your feedback in tons of disclaimers or qualifiers (or heaven forbid, use the dreadful "feedback sandwich"), your message will get watered down or lost entirely. If you skip the "O" (Often) and talk about something that happened last quarter, it doesn't matter how well you deliver your feedback, it's too late for them to course correct.

THE IMPORTANCE OF RELATIONSHIPS

Late in my tenure on the high yield team at Goldman Sachs, we got a new manager and he started doing things very differently. A lot of us were resistant to the changes. There was a fair amount of water cooler talk going on, a lot of bitching and moaning behind closed doors.

I started connecting with this clique of more senior colleagues who were so cynical they almost made it into a sport. They were having an impact on me—specifically, on how much I bitched and moaned. One day, another coworker pulled me aside.

"You know what, Shani, this is really none of my business, but I want to tell you anyway, in case it's helpful. I've noticed a few times lately that you're speaking rather publicly with some cynicism. I would just ask yourself what impact that could have on your career. I've been around this block before, so I would encourage you to just keep working hard as you always have, and adjust to the changes instead of bucking them. But that's just my two cents; you can take it or leave it."

I remember it vividly to this day because of how courageous it was for him to give me that feedback. I was touched that he had cared enough to say something, and it surely made an impact on me. I didn't want to be perceived as a cynical, non-team player. I thought, "Damn it, I'm the culture-carrier around here; how'd I let this happen?" His feedback/forward resonated with an intrinsic motivation around how I wanted to be perceived and a more extrinsic motivation around the career trajectory I had in mind for myself. It was extremely valuable then and remained with me well into the future.

Sometimes, the hardest feedback to give is when there's nothing in it for you, as was the case here. My attitude had very little impact on his performance, nor did I report to him. He was just a fellow colleague who cared enough about me to say something. That's what really mattered: he cared.

I might have received this feedback differently if I'd had a contentious relationship with him, but I already had good rapport. That's why Chapter 4 is so important. If you already have a communicative relationship built upon trust and mutual respect, when you need to have to have a tough talk or deliver difficult feedback, it will be received far more positively. Oh, and by the way, it will also be much easier for you to say it.

TOOLS FOR YOUR BETTER BOSS BELT: THE SIP™ MODEL

Following the wine theme (why not?), the SIP™ model is about delivering feedback/forward continuously—in sips, rather than in Costco-sized vats. Better bosses deliver feedback that is timely, not allowing it build up until they explode.

I believe we can all think back to a time when we've held back on feedback, even in a personal relationship, until we finally just blew up with the stress of it. When this happens, we often shoot a litany of incidents that happened months or years ago into the conversation like arrows. To add insult to injury, they're probably completely unrelated to what just transpired. That's what happens when we don't sip feedback. That's projectile vomiting feedback.

Sipping feedback is much more effective. With no further ado, I present to you eager Better Bosses, the SIP™ Model for Effective Feedback/Forward:

S **is for Situation.** Describe the situation or behavior you observed and provide examples. This keeps the feedback neutral and direct. Describe the behavior you observed without use of potentially judgmental or inflammatory adjectives. Instead of saying, "You're distracted," which is a judgment, say instead, "I noticed that you were on your phone a lot during the meeting." Instead of, "You're nervous and insecure," how about "I noticed you were speaking rapidly and using a lot of filler words." The proposed alternatives contain details that can't be disputed; they're concrete behaviors that were observed.

I **stands for Impact.** This is the point at which you share the impact this observed behavior had on you, the team, the organization, the client, and so on. The "Interests" piece from the GRIP™ model will often show up here. In describing the impact the observed behavior had on others, you'll often activate some of the intrinsic motivations this person strives for and, thus, trigger a realization of how they weren't honored with the behavior.

Let's say Steve's intrinsic motivation is autonomy and, as such, he doesn't like to be micromanaged. You have observed there are errors in virtually every deliverable he's turned in lately, so you articulate that to Steve. You might then say, "The impacts were duplicate work for a few of your colleagues, and some incorrect numbers were used in proposals. I've got to tell you, this makes me want to double-check all your numbers for the first time since I've hired you. Tell me, what's going on for you?" This approach gets right to the heart of his motivation around autonomy. Steve likes working independently and doesn't want to be micromanaged, so chances are, from this feedback he'll realize, "Oh, shit! I'm not upholding my end of the autonomy bargain!"

P **is for Possibilities**. This is the overtly feedforward part of the SIP model. It's all about where and how you'd like to see the other person grow and develop. In addition to sharing your vision for what's possible, be truly interactive here with questions like, "What could you do differently?" or "How will you approach this next time?" Possibilities can be very broad, but it's essentially a two-way discussion of "What now?"

Remember, SIP™ can be utilized with just as much impact for positive feedback/forward. For example,

Situation: "The conference you organized was a huge success! The content was timely and well-received, the speakers you selected added interesting new perspectives, and the logistics were flawless."

Impact: "It really increased our customers' confidence in our firm and raised our profile as thought leaders in the industry. And because you were all over this, I was free to focus on another strategic project. I can't thank you enough."

Possibilities: "I can see you managing an even bigger event next year. What other high-profile events are on your radar screen to quarterback?"

You can see how much richer that feedback is, in contrast to, "That conference was great." This type of feedback/forward is going to make a difference.

Better Boss Baby Steps:

Give Frequent, Balanced
Feedback and Feedforward

› Articulate specific details next time you deliver positive feedback.

› Use the SIP™ Model to have a feedback/forward conversation.

› Give feedback you've been avoiding. Remember, it's a way to develop others and improve results.

SIX
[As a Better Boss, I commit to:]

USE TIME WISELY

SIX

[As a Better Boss, I commit to:]

USE TIME WISELY

"It's not enough to be busy, so are the ants. The question is, what are we busy about?"
– Henry David Thoreau

IN THE GRAND SCHEME of things, success is ultimately the intersection of a great strategy, executed well. Simply put, great strategy is doing the right things, and execution is doing things right. A poor strategy executed well is not going to be effective, and a great strategy executed poorly is going to be tepid at best. Teams and organizations led by better bosses thrive by developing and communicating a brilliant strategic plan, and then leading people to execute it brilliantly.

There are prerequisites to brilliant strategy. Much as we talked about in Chapter 1 relative to individuals, a cohesive mission, vision, and set of values are also foundational for organizations. Without them, we're scattered. It's imperative to have a clear direction for our business—that North Star for people to follow.

Let's examine the mission, vision, and values of The Better Boss Project as an illustration. Our mission is pretty simple: To inspire as many people as possible to live and lead with no regrets. It's why we exist, and intentionally covers a lot of ground, relating to a lot of people in a lot of places in a lot of contexts.

The aspirational vision for The Better Boss Project is to become a viral movement that stirs people all around the world to become better bosses, to employ better bosses, and to groom better bosses. The vision also involves people speaking the common Better Boss Project language, using our tools, and having pithy Better Boss posters up in conference rooms and offices. Companies that have had Better Boss training for their managers and leaders will get The Better Boss Project official seal of approval to use in their marketing and recruiting materials, with the aim that they'd leverage it much like a Fortune magazine "Best Companies to Work For" endorsement.

Everyone on our team has heard the mission and vision ad nauseam, and they are completely enrolled. They want to be part of it and share it. They're also really aligned with our core corporate values of healthy relationships, lifelong learning, unforgettable fun, zesty passion, limitlessness, and clean A.I.R The mission, vision, and values are clearly communicated on our website to current and potential clients, partners, and other external constituents, and we hope they echo loudly in this book.

Working through how to develop our own mission, vision, and values is beyond the scope of this book, but I will prompt you to evaluate your own:

› Do you have a mission, long-term vision, and set of values?

> › If so, when were they created, and are they still relevant and representative of the:
>   › Organization as it exists now?
>   › Current and prospective political, economic, social, technological, environmental, and legal climates?
>   › Culture of your organization as it stands now?
>   › Competitive landscape as it exists now?

Of course, once you have developed or revitalized your mission, vision, and values, communicate them openly and enthusiastically to everyone on the team. That clears the path for a regular and rigorous strategic planning process. One day soon, the gifted technologists at Google will no doubt work on developing a crystal ball. But until that time, we mere mortals must rely on the power of thoughtful and meticulous planning to increase our odds of success at important yet uncertain junctures like formulating strategy.

EXECUTING YOUR STRATEGIC PLAN ONE BITE AT A TIME

The process by which effective strategic planning is accomplished would fill another volume, and I don't delve into it here. But once you've completed strategic planning, break the components down into smaller executable elements, each one with SMART goals attached. SMART stands for Specific, Measurable, Attainable, Realistic, and Time-bound, and assures goals are clear and contain measures for success.

As you're cascading the output of strategic planning and continuously communicating about key priorities, help your team eat the proverbial elephant one bite at a time, as the joke quips. It's easy for people to feel overwhelmed by big initiatives and projects and become frozen in a place of fear, indecision, or both.

This is a place where coaching (see Chapter 4) is going to be extraordinarily helpful. Remember the DISCUSS model? It's designed to help people eat that elephant one bite at a time. DISCUSS ends with "Steps" and "Schedule" so the conversation wraps up with a keen focus on the next actions your coachee needs to take to move forward on what Jim Collins and Jerry Porras call BHAGs (Big, Hairy, Audacious Goals) in their book Built to Last. Every day that we make progress, we can look back through the rearview mirror, and it doesn't take long before we see the cumulative benefits of taking small actions every single day.

One oft-overlooked aspect of execution is your team's collaboration tools. How are they connecting, collaborating, sharing information, communicating, and managing projects? The cloud is full of excellent tools for these purposes, so find ones your people will utilize and equip them with proper training to do so. As a better boss, it's your responsibility to make sure your team has the right tools at their disposal to use *their* time wisely.

Some organizations are so serious about using time wisely that new roles have been created. For example, Shopify has an official Director of Getting Shit Done, and the Czar of Bad Systems role at Hootsuite has the authority to fix processes—anywhere within the company—that aren't working. Those are my kind of people!

THE MAGIC OF "YES, AND..."

Many people think that working long hours and getting lots of little things done is the epitome of being productive. But that's a fallacy. Productivity is not getting more things done; it's getting the right things done. Productivity is balancing the urgent and the important, a concept made famous in a 1954 speech by President Dwight D. Eisenhower. For better bosses, the "right things" are all the activities that help you, your team, and your organization achieve their goals.

One of the most important ways to improve your productivity is to say "No" more often (see the bullet on saying "No" in the Self-Care section of Chapter 1). I'm very much a realist and recognize that sometimes you literally can't say "No" to some things. In those cases, try "Yes, and..." instead. For example, "Yes, I can take that on and...

...to free up some time for it, let's sit down and reprioritize other projects."

...to get it done on that timeline, let's talk about where we can modify some other deadlines."

...let's discuss the additional resources we'll need to be successful."

As you can see, the "Yes, and..." technique involves maintaining focus on your own key initiatives while still being flexible and solutions-oriented to pivot when necessary.

YOUR INBOX DOES NOT EQUAL YOUR OUTPUT

One thing I encourage people to say "No" to more often is email. I'm a leadership consultant and coach and don't pretend to be a psychotherapist. But what I do know is that for many people email has become addictive—habitual and unconscious—to the detriment of productivity. As with other harmful fixations, it diverts attention away from doing the things that really matter. Most people receive hundreds of emails per day, and that kind of interruption is simply not practical, let alone productive.

I am a recovering email addict myself, so I'm in a good position to testify that you can overcome the addiction. First though, learn to recognize the signs:

› Do you jump right to your inbox like one of Pavlov's dogs every time your computer chimes or smartphone vibrates?
› Do you feel the compulsion to reply to emails as soon as they come in?
› Do you frequently feel as though you accomplished nothing in your work day beside email?
› Do you rely on email as a to-do list and storage area?

If you answered "Yes" to any of these questions, you may be prioritizing email over responsibilities that are more mission-critical. Here are five suggestions I've found effective in shifting one's relationship with email from master to servant:

1. **Embrace the idea that email is not full of emergencies.** Important information, yes. But life-threatening crises, highly unlikely. Use email for important but non-urgent matters, and

align with your team and other people with whom you have regular email correspondence on a more suitable method for communicating the urgent, such as a phone call, text, or face-to-face. You can still be responsive to email (but in a more reasonable timeframe than the moment it hits your inbox), and you're freed up to focus on more essential, strategic, and thoughtful endeavors.

2. **Turn off chimes, vibrations, and icons that interrupt to announce new emails.** Every interruption, including email, costs you valuable time for the mind to refocus and gain the same level of concentration you had before the interruption. Imagine the time you're wasting even by merely glancing up in response to a chime broadcasting every non-urgent incoming message.

3. **Manage your time from forty thousand feet, not ground level.** American author Robert Heinlein once said, "In the absence of clearly defined goals, we become strangely loyal to performing daily acts of trivia." Unless your job solely revolves around your inbox and immediate email responsiveness, spending all day on email is as trivial as it gets. If you aren't focusing on your ongoing big-picture goals, email is an easy way to delude yourself into thinking you're busy. Instead, process email in batches at role-appropriate intervals throughout the day, and manage response time expectations accordingly.

4. **Don't use your inbox as a to-do list.** I'm guessing you already keep track of to-dos in at least one other place, so why kill hours of time scrolling through endless emails for needle-in-the-haystack action items? Turning an email into a task to complete

later is one convenient strategy to help you avoid "living" in your inbox. There are many exceptional cloud-based task apps out there, or the old-fashioned paper list still works too.

5. **Wash, rinse, repeat.** If you are unhappy with the amount of time you spend distracted by email, be willing to try something different. But be aware that it will take discipline and repetition because, as we've pointed out previously, any new behavior takes consistent practice.

Shayna Hughes, CEO of Learning as Leadership, instituted a mere one-week email ban in 2012, and some of the observations she shared in a subsequent Forbes article effectively sum up the benefits: "Many people mistake urgent e-mail activity for productivity, but that stressful busy-ness is invariably tactical and rarely strategic and creative. The decrease in stress from one day to the next was palpable. So was our increase in productivity. This was when I grasped the most damaging cost of thoughtless email: It prevents us from doing our best work."

As I always ask clients who struggle with email: "Will you get that promotion, raise, or bonus because you were trigger-happy on email, or because you over-delivered on big goals, quarterbacked key initiatives, and led your team to new levels of success?"

UNDERSTANDING THE BUSINESS IS A SECRET PRODUCTIVY WEAPON

One reality I don't often hear mentioned in discussions of time management is the extent to which your team's understanding of the business impacts productivity. A lot of companies don't train their non-financial employees to truly comprehend how the various functional areas interrelate, or how the business makes money. I see a lot of unnecessary wheel spinning because Marketing isn't coordinating with Operations, or Finance doesn't understand the needs of the Engineering team. That's the sound of time (and money) being wasted!

Better bosses in any functional area need at least a basic understanding of how the business of their organization works. The team should be able to relate how their roles fit into and impact their organization's and/or their clients' business outcomes and financial performance.

I feel so strongly about that competency that I developed a standalone workshop to help solve for this glaring knowledge gap. And it doesn't "taste like chicken;" in other words, it's far from boring and bland. Rather, in typical Better Boss style, it takes a dry and potentially complex topic and serves it in pleasing and easily digestible bites of only the most essential morsels, topped with a hearty ragu of playfulness and relevance.

If time is devoted to educating everyone in the organization to speak more credibly about the business with internal and external constituencies, there is no doubt productivity will improve.

Better Boss Baby Steps:

· ·

Use Time Wisely

› Check the relevance of your organization's and/or team's mission, vision, and values and update if necessary.

› Help someone on your team eat their elephant or BHAG in smaller bites.

› Replace "No" with "Yes, and…"

› Try using a cloud-based task app to manage your to-do list instead of relying on your inbox.

› Learn how your organization and/or your customers make money if you don't already know.

SEVEN
[As a Better Boss, I commit to:]

FAIL FORWARD

SEVEN

[As a Better Boss, I commit to:]

FAIL FORWARD

"We are all failures—at least the best of us are."
—J.M. Barrie, playwright and author of Peter Pan

IN ESSENCE, "FAILING FORWARD" means using honest mistakes as opportunities to learn. It holds a spirit of continuous improvement, rather than blame or shame. There is a big difference between honest mistakes and failures due to apathy or malice. Unfortunately, when managers lump "good" failures in with the toxic kind, what typically results is a collective fear of failure that is palpable on their teams.

Failing forward is the only way to encourage innovation and creativity. Anyone who has ever been successful at anything meaningful wears the badge of failure; failure is our greatest teacher. From Einstein to Edison, from professional athletes to renowned composers, from babies learning to crawl to the best

Fortune 500 CEOs, they've all learned from their failures along the way.

THE DRAMA AND EMPOWERMENT TRIANGLES

Time and time again, we find ourselves in the failure-oriented Drama Triangle, consisting of the Villain, the Victim, and the Hero.

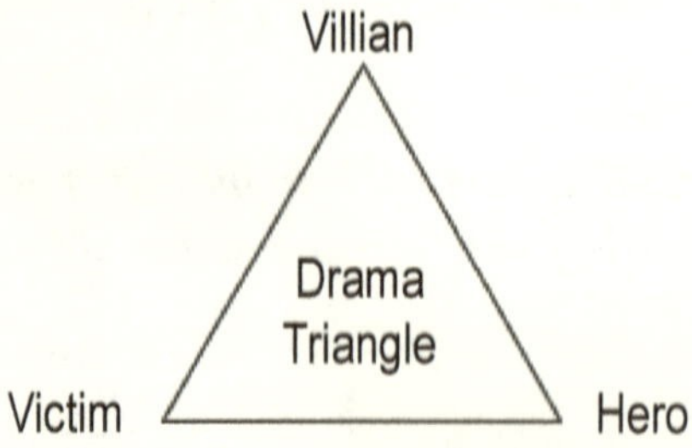

We've got a boss who shows up like a *villain*; he's an asshole who does not view failure as a learning and growth mechanism. We're scared to piss him off with even an innocent mistake, so we become a *victim*. Then we look for a *hero*, for someone to ride in on a proverbial white horse—whether that's a mentor, a new boss, a spouse, or a colleague. However, relying on a noble hero for rescue only serves to keep the victim dependent and extends further permission to fail. As we like to say in Miami, "That's no bueno!" Remember "It's always up to me" from Chapter 2? Only the victim can save himself from the villain, by stepping in powerfully as his or her own hero.

In the worst-case scenario played out with the Drama Triangle, employees hide and/or lie about mistakes and failures.

Trust is nonexistent, and the consequences of a culture like that can be catastrophic—the Enron-variety of catastrophic.

A preferable triad is the Empowerment Triangle.

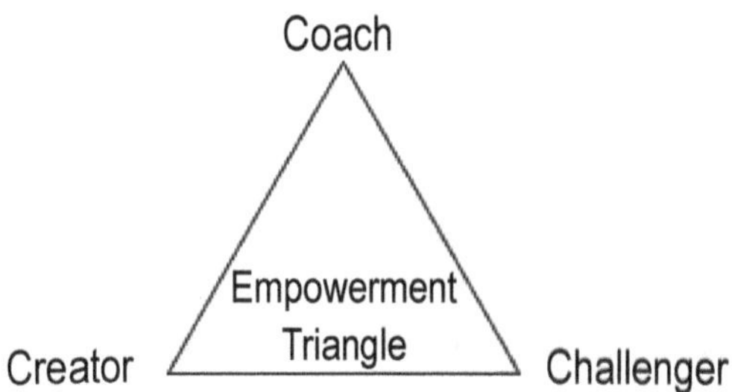

It features the boss as a *coach* instead of a villain, helping people rise to the challenges that are in front of them. Employees are *creators*, not victims, because they've got the support needed to innovate. Instead of needing a hero to rescue them, employees are looking for somebody to be a *challenger*, to propel them to even greater heights.

That's the Fail Forward context.

If you're a boss reading this book, you can influence in which triangle you and your people operate. It all depends on how you respond to failure—theirs and your own.

As an employee, you might be used to feeling like the victim, but you have power too. It's hard for your boss to be your coach if you react defensively to feedback. And you must be accountable and rise to new challenges. We all have a part to play for this empowerment triangle to work.

THREE KINDS OF FAILURE

Speaking for myself, I differentiate failures in three distinct categories.

1. **I f**ked up**. I knew better. Maybe I took a shortcut. In extreme cases, it feels horrible because I made a mistake that was directly opposed to my value system, and I knew it in my gut even if it didn't register in my brain. As a better boss of yourself and others, these are often the best learning experiences, so examine them closely. (Note: a subcategory here encompasses mistakes that are illegal, immoral, malevolent, and/or just downright intolerable. Those require swift disciplinary action.)

2. **Carelessness**. I was rushing, or perhaps I was distracted, and I made an honest mistake. It's embarrassing, but it's not fatal. The world isn't going to end. The production line isn't going to halt. The product isn't going to not sell. But I know I could have done better. That's when I need to coach myself or seek coaching from others to help figure out what was distracting me. What got in my way that caused me to lose focus and make a careless error? How can I develop a better quality control system to clear the way the next time I am rushed or distracted?

3. **Creative failure**. It's well-intentioned. I was trying to be imaginative and troubleshoot a problem in a way nobody else had before. I was trying to innovate and make something new. I took a thoughtful risk, and sometimes those just don't work out. Better bosses don't fault creative failures in themselves and others; instead, they celebrate them. When we try our best, honor our values, and take smart risks to innovate, we should

feel good about that! We extract nuggets of gold as we dig for the learning in such failures.

When *you* fail as a better boss, before you leap into self-sabotage mode, think about your failure. Analyze it. Was it careless and you just need to improve your focus? Or was it you at your best, and you should you be proud of how you embraced risk? When others fail, better bosses lead people through the same thoughtful examination, coaching them so their failures don't become derailments to future performance.

GETTING FIRED FROM PLUM TV

This next part is tough for me. It's not an easy story for me to share with the world. But I've processed it enough to see the lessons in it, and if it can help anyone else out there, I will get over my lingering embarrassment.

I was fired from that job I mentioned earlier as the general manager at Plum TV in Vail. It came as a huge surprise to me, because it happened out of the blue less than a month after I had received a glowing performance review from the president of the company. As a startup, the station had also received numerous awards and accolades since I'd joined.

When the news was delivered, I laughed at first because I literally thought it was a joke. Then I was shocked, followed shortly thereafter by anger. In retrospect, I have been able to piece together what happened. There was a staffer in his early 20s working for me, and we did not see eye-to-eye on most things—to put it mildly. When I think back, I readily acknowledge that I was not a great boss to him. I didn't like him, and I treated him differently than others on my team. On more than one occasion, I made the mistake of getting badly triggered in response to something he said or did. I don't know exactly what episode tipped the scale, but he reported it to the owner of the company, and they fired me. Just like that. My open and inappropriate disdain for this kid had trumped my performance.

As I confessed, this isn't an easy story for me to tell. I'm not proud of it. But I believe in failing forward, and this is a failure from which I learned a great deal. To name a few of those lessons, I now pay far more attention to the impact I have on people I may not connect with on a personal level. I aim to be more consistent with my employees; it doesn't matter who likes me and whom I like, it's my job to treat all people with respect and fairness. My ego took a temporary beating on this one, but I became a much better boss as a result.

A FAILURE IN BUSINESS

Getting fired wasn't my only failure, though. Not by a long shot. A few years ago, my husband and I made an investment in a healthy snack vending business, and it was a stupendous failure! We lost a lot of money. We completely overestimated the demand in the market for the product, and we had to shut the venture down in less than a year.

I was certainly upset about losing so much money, not to mention the fact that we had expended a great deal of time and effort to get the business up and running. Yet, I also felt it had been a well-intentioned decision. It wasn't negligent. When we made the decision, we made it based on some values that we hold dearly, not the least of which are nutrition and wellness. We wanted to deliver greater availability in healthier snack choices. Contrary to other mistakes I've made over the years, I spent a lot less time flagellating myself about this one. Indeed, making the *wrong decision for the right reasons* doesn't feel too bad at all.

"YES, AND..." REVISTED

In improvisational acting, one of the long-standing rules of the art is to always say "YES! And..." then creatively add on. If your scene partner comes in and says, "Grandma, that pie you're baking looks delicious," well, you now need to be Grandma, and you need to be baking pie. "Yes, and..." *builds on* what people have said and done *instead of tearing it down*. Earlier in the book, we recommend "Yes, and..." as an alternative to saying "No" outright. As a better boss channeling your inner improv actor, it's also a great tool for discussing and processing failure.

Sadly, it's more common to hear "No, but..." out in the world. "No, but..." automatically puts people on the defensive. It shuts down creativity and innovation, which is exactly the opposite of what we want and need from people. A milder, but still insidious, version is "Yes, but..." Either way, the "but" feels like you're being cut off at the knees.

I love "Yes, and...". It applies to just about anything, and especially to the technique of failing forward. Here are some simplistic examples of how "Yes, and..." can reframe failure into failing forward, all said without judgment, frustration, or blame:

I failed. "Yes, I blew that sales call. And this is what I learned and what I'll do differently next time."

You failed. "Yes, you blew that sales call. And let's use this as an opportunity to debrief and set you up for success next time. What did you learn? What might you do differently next time?"

We failed. "Yes, we blew that pitch. And let's first acknowledge all the time and hard work that we collectively put into this complex RFP process. There's a lot of great learning in this experience that we can use to set ourselves up for success next time. Where did we knock it out of the park? Where did we fail to deliver what they were looking for? What could we have done differently?"

Incidentally, "Yes, and..." is also just a wonderful conversational tool in general that I encourage people to embrace in their vocabulary in any context. In *Sell or Be Sold*, Grant Cardone explains that the first thing you should do with clients is agree with them, and then add on whatever else you want to say. This technique doesn't make other people wrong; rather, it invites them in.

TOOLS FOR YOUR BETTER BOSS BELT: THE 4 P'S FOR COACHING PEOPLE THROUGH FAILURES AND DISAPPOINTMENTS

While it's fun and rewarding to convey positive news, many leaders struggle with communicating about and managing the fallout from failure, disappointing news, or constructive criticism.

There are generally three options for dealing with such "elephants in the room": (1) choose to ignore them, (2) dance around them insufficiently, or (3) address them head-on in an open, direct, and constructive way (hmmm, how about with some clean A.I.R?). I will always recommend the last approach, accompanied by a manager-as-coach mindset.

Building on some of the tools introduced earlier, a best practice I've developed to help better bosses coach their people through such stressful situations involves a commonsense series of Four P's: Process, Probing, Perspectives, and Planning.

1. **Process.** Encourage your people to process setbacks rather than bottling them up. Disappointments obviously conjure up lots of emotion, which is energy in motion, and it's not healthy to simply brush them under the carpet. Emotion must be processed so it can move through and eventually out of us; otherwise, it literally gets stored in our bodies in such forms as tight shoulders, chronic back pain, or high blood pressure.

   While you may certainly offer to be a sounding board, most people process disappointments best in an environment outside of the office—over a bottle of wine with a spouse or trusted friend, via a run in the park, with a punching bag at the gym, on the mat at a hot yoga class, with a beloved child or pet on their lap, or maybe sitting alone in thought in a peaceful place. Better bosses give people the space and time they need, within reason.

2. **Probing.** The essence of this chapter is that we learn so much more from our frustrations and failures than we do from our successes. As such, once people have had a chance to process the emotion from a disappointment or failure, work with them to mine the valuable gems from the experience. The only real failure in any setback is to learn nothing from it and cease to

grow. Ask some probing questions to prompt meaningful self-reflection, such as:

> What do you know you do well that you want to keep doing or do more of?
> With the benefit of hindsight, what could you have done differently to realize more of what you wanted?
> How might you approach a similar situation in the future?
> Imagine you're recounting this experience a few years from now. What do you think you'd tell people that you learned?

3. **Perspectives.** A complementary approach is to help your people consider the experience from a different perspective, aside from one of distress or anxiety. We never really know the 100 percent truth behind anything that happens, and it is human nature to create stories to fill in the missing pieces in our minds. Sadly, the stories we tend to make up are often negative, self-critical, discouraging, defensive, or all the above. We can choose to adopt any mindset we want, so why not adopt one that's constructive and propels us forward? Not delusional or naïve, but grounded in some realistic possibility.

Perhaps it was a dress rehearsal for an even better opportunity coming down the pike. Or maybe it wasn't the opportunity it appeared to be on the surface. Was it a much-needed wakeup call to reevaluate what you really want? Pull out some of those self-management and ways of being tools from the first three chapters and apply them to coaching others to consider different perspectives!

> How would that best-version-of-yourself in a bottle react?
> What decision might you have made if the shoe were on the other foot, so to speak?

> › What station on your inner radio would be helpful to
> tune into right now?

4. **Planning.** Buoyed by some emotional catharsis, honest
reflections from probing questions, and some constructive
perspectives, your people will now be in a much better place
to plan next steps and revise their goals. We can't change the
past, but we can control the decisions we make and the actions
we take moving forward. Here is yet another opportunity to
DISCUSS—to help people think through their choices and get
into action.

Utilizing this 4-step approach to engage with employees who are
impacted by failures or unwelcomed changes will not only boost
their well-being, self-awareness, and productivity, but may also
increase personal accountability around their future success.
Sounds like a win-win to me!

Better Boss Baby Steps:

Fail Forward

› Recognize a situation in which you're engaged in a fruitless "drama triangle" and think about how to transform it into an "empowerment triangle."

› Notice your reaction when you fail or make a mistake. Notice your reaction when someone else fails or makes a mistake. How would you prefer to respond in both cases? What's possible then?

› Think about a recent disappointment or failure. What did you learn that will benefit you going forward?

› Try "The Four Ps" next time you coach someone through a disappointment or change.

EIGHT

[As a Better Boss, I commit to:]

MAKE DECISIONS CO-CREATIVELY

EIGHT

[As a Better Boss, I commit to:]

MAKE DECISIONS CO-CREATIVELY

"Minds are like parachutes—they only function when open."
– Thomas Dewar, witty Scottish businessman

A LOT OF LEADERS SAY THEY'RE collaborative, but in the end, any difference of opinion is often shut down and working together may even feel forced. True collaboration involves welcoming different opinions and combining ideas to come up with something more creative and impactful than anyone could have come up with individually. That's *co-creating*.

Once, I had a boss who pretended to want to know other people's opinions. On the surface, she seemed really interested. But this was a thinly-veiled cover; she almost always already had the answer preformed in her mind. If you didn't give her the answer she wanted, she would continue to fish around until you agreed. Behavior like this often turns people into robots who don't think for themselves or are afraid to voice their own opinions—not a better boss outcome.

A truly co-creative culture invites divergent viewpoints to garner better solutions. The more voices we have from different experiences, industries, functional areas, cultures, races, genders, etc., the more holistic our problem solving and decision making can be. It's true within a team, cross-functionally, across divisions, and up and down hierarchy structures.

Co-creating invites us to think beyond our own experiences and unconscious biases. It's a way to evaluate what's best for the organization, rather than what's best according to those unique yet limited personal filters we talked about in Chapter 1.

AGREEMENT VERSUS ALIGNMENT

A lot of managers want people to agree on everything, but agreement is tricky. As Aneel Karnani, professor of strategy at the University of Michigan's Ross School of Business, artfully explained, "Lack of conflict is not the same as real agreement; consensus can be a disguise for disengagement."

People may feign agreement on the outside when inside doubts or unspoken communication linger (and even worse, maybe they fester). Perhaps they don't want to have a confrontation, are afraid to speak up, or were never consulted in the first place. The vibe of agreement is one of right and wrong, black and white. That's not the best context in which to get people on-board and engaged. But this is what normally masquerades as "collaboration."

Alignment, on the other hand, means that while they may not have made the exact same decision, people feel as if they were a part of the process. Their perspectives were considered, and the decision is aligned with an overall direction about which they're passionate. Everyone's signing up for the same journey, even if they disagree about some of the specifics of the trip.

It all comes back to your organizational mission, vision, and values. First, we reaffirm alignment on those and, from that vantage point, engage in respectful, open-minded discussion. Allowing for expression of differing opinions and potentially some fierce conversation, we can more easily assimilate diverse viewpoints to co-create the best possible decisions on mission-critical matters ranging from how to restructure the business or launch a new product to how to develop talent or communicate in a crisis. Alignment creates engagement and good will in an organization that agreement simply does not.

Here's another way to think about it: Envision two mountains that originate from the same hiking trail. At some point on the path, you can either go left or go right and ascend to Peak A or Peak B. Let's say you go left and I go right, given that each of us is convinced our way is the best. When we try to collaborate while standing on two different peaks, we're literally in two different places. It'll soon be obvious that we aren't communicating well, and we're going to have to shout at each other to be heard.

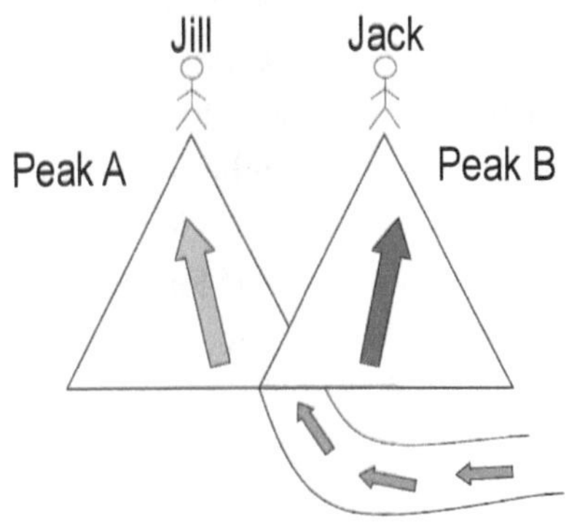

Instead, what if we descend a little, back to where the trails for the two mountains intersect and blend back into a single path? From there, we can connect on our common mission, communicate effectively, and engage in a discussion from a place of alignment. We'll decide on which mountain peak to tackle together, and, even if we employ slightly different hiking techniques en route, we'll still be focused on a shared goal.

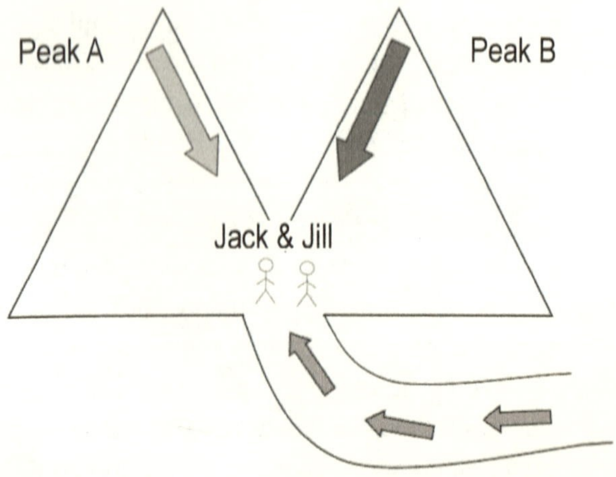

At the school where I pursued my coaching certification, The Coaches Training Institute, the rule governing our last in a series of in-person workshops was: "Everybody, nobody, everything, and nothing gets to be wrong or right." That always stands out to me as a great motto for remembering how to be co-creative when seeking alignment. It's a wonderfully non-conventional way to set an open and positive tone for a meeting during which there will undoubtedly be differences of opinion. Instead of dissimilar views being a potential deterrent to moving forward, they become desirable gifts from which to build something new and exciting, something you never would have built with closed minds and fixed stances.

HOW SHOULD I BE IN THE FACE OF CHANGE?

The 21st-century workplace can be compared to an airplane that's being built while it's in the air flying. The pace of change and continuous innovation of "newer, better, faster" is such that hardly anyone can keep up with it. In fact, a recent PwC study found that about 40 percent of jobs are likely to be automated with current technology by 2030. Certainly, many of the management tools we learned ten or twenty years ago no longer suffice.

A better boss in the face of change means *being* open-minded, resilient, decisive, and communicative. These competencies are more critical than ever before, because business leaders at every level are navigating a V.U.C.A. world. Originated by the U.S. Army War College, it means our world is characterized by Volatility, Uncertainty, Complexity, and Ambiguity. Lately, other thought-leaders have aptly been adding a "D" (for Disruption) on the end, so now we have a V.U.C.A.D. world where the only constant is change. There will always be unexpected obstacles. We will usually be armed with only imperfect information. And nobody has all the answers on their own. The skill of co-creating is a powerful offensive weapon with which better bosses can confront their V.U.C.A.D. environments.

HOUSTON'S, WE DON'T HAVE A PROBLEM!

A few years ago, I met a client at Houston's Restaurant in Boca Raton, Florida for a happy-hour drink, and we both ordered martinis. Much to our delight, after about twenty minutes of sipping our cocktails, the bartender switched out our glasses for new, freshly-chilled ones. It was unsolicited and unobtrusive. Not only were we pleasantly surprised, but as astute business women, we were also impressed. What a clever yet easy way to wow the customer and create a memorable experience.

Not to sound elitist, but I have been served cocktails at far fancier, non-chain restaurants all over the world. Yet this was the first time I had ever been given an ice-cold glass without having ordered an entirely new beverage. And suffice it to say that I'm well past the age of twenty-one, so I've had a few social drinks in my time.

While this incident may seem inconsequential, it still stands out to me because we talked about it for more than a passing moment when it happened, and both of us told other people about it later. In fact, I was so charmed that I felt compelled to call Houston's to find out if we had been served by a particularly shrewd bartender, if the glass exchange was standard operating procedure for the Boca location, or if the entirety of the chain is that attentive. The restaurant manager happened to answer the phone and informed me that, in fact, this is a refinement bar staff are encouraged to execute institutionally across all locations to distinguish their service. Kudos to the Hillstone Restaurant Group, owner of Houston's.

Like many industries, the restaurant business is insanely competitive, and Houston's landed on an effective yet low-cost way to differentiate itself at the bar. I have no idea how the idea was hatched in reality, but the story I make up is that some proactive leaders at the company assembled a group of managers, servers, bartenders, and maybe even customers in a room to co-create ways to stay relevant in an ever-changing environment.

PUPPYFORCE: A CASE STUDY IN CO-CREATING EMPLOYEE ENGAGEMENT

Salesforce's program for allowing pets at work is hardly surprising; it's called Puppyforce. But the cute name is not what differentiates it, and permitting pets at the office is not necessarily a new perk. What stands out to me is the strategically innovative way in which Salesforce went about designing their unique version of this employee benefit and the bona fide emphasis they place on building a highly-engaged workforce in general.

In a *Fortune* magazine feature, Christopher Thaczyk described how Puppyforce took shape via discussions on Chatter, their enterprise social networking platform. Incorporating feedback from employees concerned about allergies, hygiene, and noise, Puppyforce ultimately took shape as a separate soundproof workspace with rubber floors and a reservation system. Monika Fahlbusch, SVP of Global Employee Success, said, "Everybody who had concerns now raves about our solution because it really met everyone's needs."

Rather than simply dismissing an idea that has opposition or may seem irreconcilable on the surface, better bosses find ways to bridge the gaps instead. They are resourceful and solutions-oriented, like Salesforce was in this example. They're co-create, inviting people to think broadly without judging, evaluating, or making decisions until all ideas have been captured, including ones that may seem far-fetched at first glance. The idea is to create an environment that gets people to shed their typical patterns and filters to consider the situation from a variety of different perspectives. From this broad array of ideas, innovative solutions can then take shape.

TOOLS FOR YOUR BETTER BOSS BELT: GROUP DISCUSS

"We are continually faced by great opportunities brilliantly disguised as insolvable problems," said former Chrysler CEO Lee Iacocca. One approach to try when this shows up in your world is the DISCUSS model presented in Chapter 4. It's not only a framework that you can use to coach others, but it's also a tool you can use to co-create with a team. Just switch the pronouns from "you" to "we" and "us." I've seen lots of really great things happen when teams take a coaching-inspired approach to solving problems and V.U.C.A.D. challenges.

Take the time to think through the issue in a systematized way with the team. Solicit input and ideas from everyone in an orderly fashion. Create a brainstorming space where "everybody, nobody, everything, and nothing gets to be wrong or right." From there, you can come up with the next steps from a place of alignment, because everybody was involved in the discussion. Not only does this encourage shyer people to toss their ideas out there, but it also levels the playing field with those more strong-minded folks who may typically dominate in meetings and/or think they already have the right answer.

Better Boss Baby Steps:

Make Decisions Co-Creatively

› Reflect on a situation in which you and another person have metaphorically been standing on two different mountain peaks. What's possible if you both descended to a place of commonality?

› Identify a V.U.C.A.D challenge in your world and pick a few people with diverse experiences and views with whom to brainstorm ideas and co-create ways to potentially offset it.

› Use the DISCUSS™ Model to solve a problem or co-create with a group of other people.

NINE

[As a Better Boss, I commit to:]

HOLD MEETINGS THAT DON'T SUCK

NINE

HOLD MEETINGS THAT DON'T SUCK

"Excellence is to do a common thing in an uncommon way."
– Booker T. Washington, educator, author, and civil rights
leader

WE SPEND AN UNFATHOMABLE amount of time in meetings. Some of my clients literally have meetings from 8:00 A.M. to 6:00 P.M. Thus, they're sidelined into doing their "real work" early in the morning or at night, cutting into dinner and family time. The old joke that says, "We're having a meeting to talk about our meeting," is not a joke in some organizations.

We all know the stereotype of the bad meeting: It doesn't start on time. It doesn't end on time. There is no agenda. People go off on tangents; no one sticks to the goals of the meeting—if there are any. There is unequal participation. There are people sitting around the table not paying attention, on their phones doing email or playing Words with Friends. Nothing actionable comes out of the meeting. They're time-sucks, and boring time-sucks at that. Watching a movie would probably be a better use of company time; at least morale might go up!

A better boss knows that meetings need to be a good use of people's time.

THE WORK BEFORE THE MEETING

The first tenet of holding meetings that don't suck is this: The meeting starts before the assembly itself! The leader needs to be really clear on the purpose of the meeting. Better bosses hold meetings to accomplish the following objectives:

> Make decisions
> Move the ball forward on an initiative or project
> Communicate unusual news
> Build relationships
> Inspire and/or celebrate a milestone or achievement
> Co-create

Meetings should not be held to update each other about shit that could have come in an email or in one-on-ones. Don't just meet because you're a committee; meet because you've got a reason.

When you're the meeting leader, consider what outcomes you're aiming for and what impact you want to make. If the person leading the meeting isn't clear on the intended outcome, the meeting's sure to meander. Determining the impact you want a meeting to have on participants also lends direction and intentionality. Do you want them to leave energized? Focused?

Excited? Determined? Such preparation on your part will frame everything else you do before, during, and after a meeting.

Once you know the outcome and the impact you want, only then can you put together a meaningful agenda, rather than just defaulting to the one you've always used—or, worse, skipping an agenda altogether. The outcome and impact may also dictate when you schedule a meeting that's non-recurring; be strategic about the optimal time for the subject matter to be discussed.

WHO NEEDS TO ATTEND?

The next thing to consider is who really needs to be present at this meeting. Oftentimes, people are invited out of politeness or politics, or maybe they just were never removed from the meeting invite list after their presence became optional or unnecessary. Coordinating an excessive number of people for a meeting can be a staggering feat. Who absolutely must be at this meeting, and whom could you live without?

The most left-brained way to figure this out is to do an ROI for all the people for the meeting. Who is in the meeting? What are their annual salaries? If you don't know, estimate. What's the cost of all those people spending an hour in a room for that meeting? What's the opportunity cost of those same people not being elsewhere that would be a higher and better use of their time? Do we accomplish enough in the meeting to justify the expense?

Better bosses are selective about who is invited to meetings, and they specify whose attendance is required versus optional.

THE INVITATION

Have you ever received a meeting invitation that doesn't even suggest what the meeting is about? I decline those meetings, to be honest. Who has time to attend a meeting about nothing? Even if it's a standing weekly staff meeting or a monthly marketing meeting, let attendees know what to expect. And if it's a one-time meeting, don't make the recipients guess. Tell them what it's about! That knowledge gives people a chance to prioritize their attendance at the meeting, prepare if they plan to go, and think about what they want to contribute.

On the 1960s' television show Dragnet, the detectives always said, "Just the facts, Ma'am. Just the facts." Remember that when you're inviting people to your meeting: include the FAACTS in the calendar invitation. Yes, you know me by now; it is indeed another acronym. No charge for the extra "A."

F **is for the Four Ws**: Who, What, When, and Where. Those are the most basic details: Who is on the "To" line, What's the meeting about, and When/Where will it take place? That sets the tone and gives people the information they'll need.

The first *A* is for Agenda. Put an agenda in the meeting request, even if it's just a preliminary one. This just helps attendees generally know what you're hoping to accomplish. If you can't answer that basic question, you shouldn't be scheduling the meeting.

The second *A* is for Actions. What, if any, actions are required of the participants in advance of the meeting? Are there some materials participants need to have reviewed before they arrive? Is there anything you need them to prepare, such as reports or stats? Give people advance notice so there's enough lead time to do the work.

C **stands for Chairperson**. Who's in charge? Sometimes the person who is actually leading the meeting is not the same person who sent the invitation. Whether that's an administrative assistant who coordinates calendars for more than one manager, or the normal leader is on vacation, clarify for everyone who's running the meeting.

T **stands for Team.** Which team members' presence is required and which is optional? While it would be valuable to have the optional attendees, the meeting can take place without them. The last thing you want is for everyone to get together, only to realize that the person whose sign-off you need is not there. That just means you'll have to schedule another meeting.

S stands for Supporting Materials. For example, if you requested in the "Actions" bullet that attendees review sales figures or a research report, make sure it's attached or clearly indicate where the relevant materials can be found. That will save time and confusion before the meeting.

BASIC RULES FOR EFFECTIVE MEETINGS

We all know meetings should start on time, but have you given space to those who have meetings back to back? Some organizations have such big campuses that if meetings are scheduled for an hour and they're back to back, a solid ten to fifteen minutes may be necessary to travel from Building A to Building F. One simple way to accommodate travel time is to schedule forty-five minutes instead of one hour. Shorter meetings keep you that much more focused, and when you're crystal clear coming into a meeting, you can probably accomplish in forty-five minutes what might have once taken an hour or longer.

At the outset of the meeting, articulate the purpose and intended outcome. Set the tone and pay continuous attention to whether you're landing the impact you had in mind.

One of the easiest ways meetings get derailed is when people surface something that's important but off topic for this meeting. Easy fix. Ask someone to record such things in a "parking lot" for future follow-up so you can keep the meeting on track.

Ending a meeting effectively is equally as important. Summarize what the next steps and timelines are for anyone who has committed to a follow-up action. Check in one last time to see if your actual impact matched your intent. If you were shooting for optimistic enthusiasm, did people leave with that attitude? Or did they leave with anxiety and stress? If the impact created does not match what you intended, take a step back and reassess how you ran the meeting.

Of course, none of this means you can't be flexible! There is a difference between adjusting based on what needs to happen in the moment and letting the meeting get sidetracked over an irrelevant topic. Better bosses can walk that line.

AFTER THE MEETING: HOLDING YOUR TEAM ACCOUNTABLE

And now, for the last vital step: the post-meeting work. The meeting doesn't end when the meeting adjourns.

Better bosses hold people accountable to what they committed to in the meeting. There is no one right way to hold people accountable; there are as many approaches to accountability as there are people on your team. What's universally important is aligning on methods of communication and utilizing tools that work for both parties, not just you, to ensure accountability.

VIRTUAL MEETINGS

No treatise on meetings would be complete without a nod to the virtual meeting. So many meetings these days do not take place gathered around a table in a conference room; people participate from all over the world. What nuances do you need to think through when it comes to being a better boss in a virtual meeting?

If you've ever held or attended a virtual meeting and want to laugh out loud, check out the Tripp and Tyler satire, a Zoom ad titled "Video Conference Call in Real Life." As the former COO of a company in which all our folks worked from home offices, I surely did! I can't help with bandwidth challenges, but based on my experiences, I can wholeheartedly recommend a few best practices for conducting meetings that will at least figuratively connect a highly-distributed team.

› **Maintain a professional set-up**. Using a video platform—instead of voice-only— is obvious. People should be able to make eye contact with each other and read non-verbal cues just as if they were sitting in the same room. Not only will that minimize the inevitable multi-tasking that occurs when people "hide" behind a computer screen, but it also fosters an environment of connection and mutual respect. This means all participants should take care to ensure these best practices:
  › Video cameras are at or close to eye level and framing them nicely.
  › Lighting is conducive to being seen clearly.
  › Distractions (i.e. kids, pets, devices, background noise) are minimized in advance.
  › All the materials they need to participate are handy.

› **Maximize technology tools.** Utilize the features available on your video conferencing platform to focus people's attention, pique visual interest, and boost co-creation. Take full advantage of highlighters, drawing tools, white boards, chat rooms, screen sharing, and other interactive features.

› **Encourage broad participation**. With the above technology basics at your disposal, it's even easier to actively engage team members the way we've already mentioned as best practices for face-to-face meetings. Don't accept less participation just because the meeting is virtual!

Better Boss Baby Steps:

Hold Meetings That Don't Suck

> Be more selective and communicative about meeting attendance – for yourself and others.

> Send out a more thorough invitation to an upcoming meeting.

> Attempt to finish a meeting that's normally 60-minutes in 45-minutes.

> Boost active participation, with video if possible, on your next virtual meeting.

TEN

[As a Better Boss, I commit to:]

SUSTAIN THE RIGHT CULTURE

TEN

[As a Better Boss, I commit to:]

SUSTAIN THE RIGHT CULTURE

"Culture eats strategy for breakfast."
– Peter Drucker, management guru

YOU CAN HAVE THE GREATEST strategy in the world, but if you don't have a culture that supports the execution of that strategy, it's not going to happen.

A formal definition of culture is a set of embedded, collective practices and beliefs which reinforce behavior and conduct. In practice, it's the collection of stories we tell ourselves about what is valued, expected, and accepted. Culture is informed by and influenced by all the systems in place, such as the org structure, strategies, policies, processes and procedures, communication protocols, and resource allocation. But culture is more informal and less concrete than those associated systems. That's partly why it's so hard to manage.

Just like setting the tone in a meeting, culture sets the tone for teams and the entire organization, and it's got to start at the top.

THE STORY OF MY FIRST BETTER BOSS

My first job out of college was with Chase Manhattan Bank in their esteemed Management Development Program (MDP). It was one of the best of any commercial bank, and the year-long program included courses in economics, finance, accounting, bank operations, and marketing, taught by top professors from Columbia and NYU. They basically paid us to get an MBA. At Chase, I got my first taste of the positive impact a better boss can make.

In addition to the classroom time and team projects, the program also involved three hands-on job rotations. I did one rotation in credit card marketing, where I designed the very first activation sticker placed on Chase credit cards and ensured the 1-800-FLOWERS advertising insert made it into your January statement—before Valentine's Day. I know, I know—impressive work indeed! My other rotations were in investment services and commercial lending.

Cheryl Tierney was my boss for the commercial lending rotation in Connecticut, and she was a spitfire. Barely five-foot tall, she was more powerful in her energy and presence than anyone I'd ever known. She was smart, driven, and engaging— she was awesome. I wish all young people had a boss to

In 1992, with my Chase team in Connecticut, led by Cheryl Tierney.
Diminutive in height only, she's on the far left kneeling on a barstool.

whom they could really look up the way I had with Cheryl so early in my career.

Chase had acquired two small banks in Connecticut, and Cheryl was part of the team working to integrate them into the system. The big project she assigned to me and an MDP peer was to educate the new marketplace about Chase, and she let us create and manage the entire thing. We ended up coordinating a huge sales event in just under eight weeks. It was a concentrated effort involving several hundred bankers calling on thousands of customers across the entire state, during a one-day "blitz." We managed everything from logistics, to marketing, branding, and all internal and external communications. We drafted memos for the division manager; we wrote scripts for bankers to appointment-set; we even came up with team names. It was literally everything.

I was twenty-two years old at the time. It would have been so easy, and not surprising, for Cheryl to micromanage everything. It was a huge amount of responsibility-especially for unproven newbies, but she just let us run with it. This experience was my first lesson in what a great boss really looks like. Cheryl gave us room to be creative; she empowered us to take ownership; she equipped us to do a great job. While offering us an incredible amount of independence to work on this project, she was accessible if we had questions or needed support navigating politics. Cheryl had an incredible impact on me because she fostered a dynamic culture marked by high levels of empowerment, alignment, communication, accountability, and engagement. She brought out the best in people and, in return, we consistently delivered our best for her.

SAS AND GOOGLE EAT CULTURE FOR BREAKFAST...PLUS LUNCH AND DINNER

I can't tell you how many times I've heard middle managers say, "These tools are great, but the people we report to don't use them." Or, "We really should do this, but the CEO just doesn't share that value." The employees may make up the majority of the people in any given culture, but the tone is set at the top.

When Larry Page and Sergey Brin were incubating Google, they were extremely intentional about the culture they wanted to create. In a fascinating 2013 Fast Company article, Mark Crowley highlighted some of this foundational Google-y history:

"In the company's early days, long before it had thousands of workers, Larry Page and Sergey Brin set their sights on making Google a truly great place to work. Determined to attract and retain great talent, they went in search of organizations that had proven histories of caring for people, driving extraordinary innovation, and building truly remarkable brands. Ultimately, they identified the SAS Institute as being one company worth emulating."

SAS is a privately-held software company incorporated in 1976, decades before most of today's hot Silicon Valley tech companies. It's always been renowned as a great place to work, and, importantly, they also have a consistent record of performing year in and year out. In fact, revenue has increased every year since founding. Here's why:

› There's limited hierarchy and a fluid org structure.
› Employees are given a lot of autonomy.
› Developers are encouraged to pursue experimental product ideas.
› Customers' input drives software development (and, according to SAS, 80 percent of suggestions for product improvements are incorporated into the software).
› Turnover in the organization is a fraction of what's typical in the software business.
› Their business model, benefits, and unique culture continue to receive accolades. SAS has been named as a "Best Company to Work For" in Fortune's annual rankings each year since the list's inception in 1997.

The perception is that Google originated the over-the-top-employee-benefits model, but in fact, it was SAS. The company offers on-site day care (plus summer camp) for children, free routine medical services for employees and their families, a free recreation and fitness center, and onsite cafeterias. Sick days are unlimited, but the average employee takes only two. SAS successfully created and continues to maintain an environment that integrates the company's business objectives with employees' personal needs. As SAS CEO James Goodnight was quoted as saying in *Management: Inventing and Delivering Its Future*, "95 percent of a company's assets drive out the front gate every night, the CEO must see to it that they return the following day." Now you understand why SAS's culture was aspirational and inspirational for Google. As Crowley went on to explain:

> "The Google founders met personally with SAS executives and sent a team of people to its headquarters in Cary, North Carolina. Collectively, they validated their understanding that people truly thrive in their jobs—and remain loyal to them—when they feel fully supported and authentically valued. This led to the launch of plentiful perks and a culture intentionally anchored by trust, transparency, and inclusion. But in setting its sights on making employees contented, Google wasn't seeking a competitive advantage as much as it was trying to ensure its own sustainable success."

Emulating the SAS DNA is a central reason Google has been so innovative and successful. They even do an admirable job at failing forward! There's a whole arm of Google that's set up to fail: Google X, which works on problems to which there are currently no solutions. As their website explains, "We're a moonshot factory. Our mission is to invent and launch 'moonshot' technologies that we hope could someday make the world a radically better place. We have a long way to go before we can fulfill this mission, so today it's really an ambition." How incredible is that!

Page and Brin very intentionally put all these things in place to set the right cultural tone from the top. Now, Google, while surely not perfect, is the standard for what great organizational culture looks like. But not for nothing—as of this writing, they have the second biggest market capitalization of any company in the world.

"THERE'S NO CRYING IN BASEBALL" (WITH APOLOGIES TO A LEAGUE OF THEIR OWN)

While I will always maintain that culture starts at the top, that doesn't preclude those not at the top from self-regulating and reinforcing it. In March 2017, the Texas Rangers announced a surprise demotion of top-tier relief pitcher Keone Kela down to the Triple As. As reported by various sports media, Kela's "third strike" was lack of effort in a recent intra-squad practice game. This really bothered fellow players, including team leader Adrian Beltre, and they let Kela know about it in no uncertain terms. But this wasn't the first time. On several prior occasions, veteran teammates intervened when Kela's volatility on the mound led to divisiveness on the team. This was in addition to Team Manager Jeff Banister's having reproached Kela after run-ins with opponents such as the Toronto Blue Jays and Los Angeles Angels.

> "One of our competitive advantages, maybe our biggest competitive advantage, is our clubhouse culture, our atmosphere, the family that is our organization," Rangers General Manager Jon Daniels said at the time of the demotion. "Sometimes when things happen in families, you need a little time to address them. That's what's happened here."

Banister put an even finer point on it, saying, "It's not about sending a message. It's about keeping the continuity and the character and the integrity and making sure the team is moving in the same direction."

Better bosses, including "players" themselves, take action when colleagues' detrimental behavior flies in the face of the accepted culture.

"TALKIN' 'BOUT MY GENERATION"

At no time in history have we had as many generations represented in the workplace as we do now. We've still got colleagues from the Great Generation, plus Baby Boomers, Gen X, Millennials, and now Gen Z. That spans a lot of years and a multitude of different mindsets and capabilities. If managed poorly, there is also plentiful opportunity for misunderstanding and miscommunication.

Many approaches for managing, motivating, and communicating with the Great Generation and Baby Boomers—and even Gen X—don't work with Millennials and Gen Z. Learning how to harness the strengths from every generation is part of creating the fabric of a great culture.

Better bosses adapt their style to play to everyone's strengths. Turnover in the younger generations is a huge problem for organizations whose leaders are not doing this effectively. Extreme hierarchy and command-and-control culture simply don't connect with the values and motivations of Millennials and Gen Z. They're not as afraid to take risks, switch jobs, or even switch industries. Why not choose to leverage the gifts in those qualities, instead of giving up on them as employees who will be gone in a year? Smart risk-taking is an asset.

Are you inviting Millennials and Gen Zs to co-create and feel like they're part of a bigger mission? That matters to them, and it better matter to you if you want them to stay loyal to your organization. People are no longer sticking around for thirty years to get the clichéd gold watch. That's just not enough anymore. Millennials will comprise 50 percent of the workforce by 2020, and 75 percent by 2030. What steps can you take to become a better boss for all generations?

FLEXIBILITY AS A CULTURAL DYNAMIC

In February 2013, then newly-appointed Yahoo CEO Marissa Mayer made a controversial decision to recall all staffers working from home back to a physical office. "Some of the best decisions and insights come from hallway and cafeteria discussions, meeting new people, and impromptu team meetings. Speed and quality are often sacrificed when we work from home," read the internal Yahoo memo. In contrast, proponents of remote work arrangements countered with arguments such as telecommuting decreases pointless, time-wasting socialization, and telecommuters actually work more hours. Well, who is right? The answer is this: It depends.

Here's the thing—it's not about working from home versus in the office. That's too simplistic. Rather, it's about the workers themselves and their managers. Having run an all-virtual company for nearly five years, I can tell you that not all people are suited to work-from-home situations, and not all managers are equipped to supervise and hold those workers accountable. These and other factors along the human capital chain ultimately determine the efficacy of any remote work situation.

Better bosses hire people from the outset who are likely to be effective working remotely. Candidates must be prequalified during the interview process to gauge if the proposed arrangement fits their behavioral style and personality or if they need the water cooler and employee cafeteria to thrive. When staffing our virtual team, we always asked targeted questions specifically designed to assess whether applicants possessed qualities such as:

› Discipline to work from home amidst distractions and with varying amounts of daily direction or supervision
› Ability to work independently, being a self-starter and taking initiative
› Judgment to reach out for help when needed, despite being alone in a home office
› Experience in a similar work environment or culture

You may even go as far as to administer appropriate pre-hire assessments to final contenders to glean more tangible data for predicting success or failure on a highly-distributed team.

As discussed in Chapters 6 and 9, slick technology enables collaboration and on-demand communication, which are essential for boosting both camaraderie and efficiency among remote workers. Are you equipping and effectively training all your people—those who work in the office and those who don't—on the right tools to communicate early and often?

Once hired and trained, remote staffers shouldn't remain out of sight and out of mind. Following the better boss practices put forth in this book is particularly crucial with remote workers. When she consulted Yahoo's VPN logs, the data told Mayer that remote employees weren't signing in enough. This signified to her that Yahoos weren't working from home, they were *shirking* from home. But VPN logs are merely one of many ways to measure effort. Perhaps if Yahoo managers had been holding their folks accountable along the way, Mayer may not have felt the need to lay down the law by ordering everyone back to Sunnyvale.

Working from home is not a one-size-fits-all panacea, but neither was Mayer's directive to eliminate them all. Better bosses consider other flexible work alternatives beyond just working from home, as appropriate for the person and the role. Job sharing, flexible hours, compressed work weeks, part-time and part-year work, sabbaticals, and other extended leaves are among the countless options for keeping workers engaged and retaining those for whom the traditional Monday to Friday, 40- to 60-hour work week is a deal-killer. Otherwise, you risk losing some top talent and/or being unable to attract the right new talent.

This is a lesson in being thoughtful about the culture you're creating. For Google, autonomy and perks all over the place works well—but that's because Google also has a concomitant culture of results. Broad-based accountability was not happening at Yahoo. No matter which, if any, flexibility policies are adopted, better bosses ensure accountability.

SPREADING HAPPINESS AT SXSW INTERACTIVE

It was day two at the 2014 SXSW (South by South West) Interactive Conference, and complaints from conference attendees were pervasive about waiting in insufferably long lines to get into popular seminars or getting shut out entirely. Sure, I expected throngs of people keen to see Mark Cuban, Michael Dell, Shaq, or Chelsea Clinton, who were among that year's marquee speakers. But I was floored to be turned away from an obscure and clearly non-tech session titled "Make Yourself the Happiest Person on Earth." Though I was disappointed to miss the session, it was encouraging to see the large crowd of professionals drawn to a seminar on happiness.

Chade-Meng Tan led this surprisingly oversubscribed seminar on the unlikely topic of happiness at a technology conference designed to showcase new innovations, processes, and thought leadership. Admittedly, Mr. Tan is fairly well-known in the tech world, as he's a former Google engineer known for taking unique advantage of the company's policy of allowing employees to devote 20 percent of their time to passion projects. His project of choice was working on world peace. Not wearable technology, not virtual reality, not self-driving cars—yes, world peace. Not only did Google not try to dissuade him, but the course Mr. Tan designed on mindfulness, called "Search Inside Yourself," became one of the most popular classes ever taught at Google University. Subsequently, he wrote a book, did a TED Talk, and met the Dalai Lama. His current role entails teaching Googlers how to apply mindfulness techniques to their life and work in service of producing happier, healthier, and more creative employees.

This theme around happiness, employee well-being, and resultant business success popped up elsewhere in a variety of seminars from which I wasn't turned away. For example, Stew Friedman, a long-time Wharton MBA professor and Director of the Wharton Work/Life Integration Project, was a participant on a panel entitled "Man Up: Gender & the Work-Life Balance Debate." Friedman told us that he sees some of his best and brightest male and female students making career decisions that prioritize balance and non-extreme schedules over money and influence.

And speaking of influence, colorful venture capitalist and wine guru Gary Vaynerchuk gave some sage advice (with his well-known penchant for expletives) to budding technologists: "When you stop prioritizing people's f**king clout and act like a human being, you will win." This statement was made in the context of encouraging people to "pay it forward" first, as a way to get the most out of attending SXSW, i.e. what goes around comes around, and you'll be happier and more successful for it.

Then there was the key message of a session called "What's the New Having It All?" In essence, today, people want to have a job they love (at least most of the time), make some money, and do some good in the world. You don't have to read much between the lines to see that's also about happiness, both personal and on a broader scale.

Most attendees at SXSW Interactive were there to pitch their ideas and connect to possible sources of funding—or to market products to those groups of people. However, the popularity of the happiness seminar and ubiquity of related themes of balance and fulfillment tells me that today's generation of entrepreneurs may not be as willing to sacrifice every other aspect of life for their work as were their predecessors. Better bosses incorporate this knowledge into the cultures they create.

TOOL FOR YOUR BETTER BOSS BELT: TAKE YOUR VITAMINS

There is no simple, all-inclusive tool to help you create the right culture. It's complex. One thing, however, that you can always come back to as you're creating a culture, is to ask yourself, "Would I want my kid to work here?"

If the answer is "No," why not? What could you do differently? If you can't quite figure it out, think about your VITamins—the Very Important Things your organization needs, much like the vitamin regimen you take for your personal health. It's a summary checklist of better boss practices to run through if something feels a bit off.

Vitamin A **is Accountability**. Do you/team/org do what you say you'll do?

Vitamin B **is Building Bridges** (rather than keeping people separate). That's how to co-create!

***Vitamin C1* is Communication.** Are you doing it with clean A.I.R. (Authenticity, Integrity, Respect)?

***Vitamin C2* is Coaching.** Do you have a coach and are you a coach to your team?

***Vitamin D* is Development.** Are you developing yourself and other people?

***Vitamin E* is Engagement.** Are you engaged in your work, and are you creating a culture of engagement?

***Vitamin F* is Feedback/Feedforward.** Do you SIP it and provide it with PINOT flair? Are you giving both positive and constructive varieties?

***Vitamin I* is Innovation.** Do you encourage people to fail forward?

***Vitamin P* is Productivity.** Do you use your own and others' time wisely?

One person—a better boss—can change an environment. And a better environment can change everything. Living and Leading with #NoRegrets may involve taking some of the VITamins you are missing in your culture diet!

Better Boss Baby Steps:

Sustain the Right Culture

› Get honest with yourself about the culture on your team. What's one thing you could change readily to improve the culture?

› Adopt a new perspective about a colleague or friend who represents a different generation.

› Identify which "VITamins" would benefit your org/team and take action to add them in the culture diet.

CONCLUSION

MAKE THE COMMITMENT

CONCLUSION

WORKING FOR A GREAT BOSS IS AMAZING, and being a great boss...well, that feels incredible. The Better Boss Project is a starting place. It's a mirror to hold up to yourself and your leadership and to look for opportunities to improve. You may not need all of it; maybe only a few of the chapters stand out to you. Take the items you want off this Better Boss buffet and run with those.

If you do see room for improvement in all ten of these areas, remember to eat the elephant one bite at a time. No one can do all of this at once. What are you most eager to improve and/or what enhancement would make the biggest immediate positive impact? Eat that first, before you fill up on the other stuff. Pick a couple of spots, and then make some clear commitments. Make commitments to yourself, and make commitments to other people. Not only will they be able to encourage you, but they'll also be able to help hold you accountable.

For a lot of people, the first step is, in fact, Chapter 1: Get your own shit together! It will be difficult, to say the least, to develop any of the other best practices in these chapters if you don't have that sorted out. If more than one chapter resonates with you, start with the earliest one—don't work on Chapter 6 before you work on Chapter 2. They build on each other.

Then practice, practice, practice. No new habit gets traction unless it's done consistently. Do the laps. Every day.

BETTER BOSS BASICS: THE ABCS

If at any time in your journey you feel overwhelmed, just remember the ABCs of being a better boss (what, did you think you'd get away without a final acronym?):

A: **Ask questions.** Ask more curious, open-ended questions that put you in a position of coach, rather than dictator. You can do this up, down, or sideways in the organization—it doesn't have to just be you and your direct reports. Ask, ask, ask! And listen.

B: **Be human**. Remember, we're managing people. People have good days and bad days. Put yourself in their shoes, consider their perspectives, and be inclusive. Keep in mind that crucial culture question from Chapter 10: Is this an organization you'd want your kid to work at? Be human, be real, be compassionate.

C: **Check assumptions**. Are you bringing your own baggage to your management style? Are your decisions informed solely by your own filters, or are they broad-based, in the best interest of the organization and your team?

In short, better bosses understand that connection is key. Take it from Theo Epstein, President of the 2016 World Series-winning Chicago Cubs, who offered, "When people do things they weren't even sure they were capable of, I think it comes back to connection. Connection with teammates. Connection with organization. Feeling like they belong in the environment. It's a human need—the need to feel connected."

THE BETTER BOSS PROJECT AMBASSADORS

What else do The Better Boss Project ambassadors have in common? They are goal-oriented, dynamic, self-starting, and self-aware. Relationships matter to them. They want to continually learn and improve themselves as people and as leaders at work; they are open to trying new things. They know, as Einstein first suggested, that doing the same thing over and over again and expecting different results is the definition of insanity! They might work at a Fortune 500 company that offers "check-the-box" leadership development training, and it just never stuck. Or they might be young founders of a startup, or long-time entrepreneurs, or coaches in a community sports league. Regardless, they are willing to take ownership of their own personal and professional development. They understand that treating their people better will make for more delighted customers, vendors, and other stakeholders, and, ultimately, a more profitable business. But most were never taught how to do this effectively.

Better bosses know that work doesn't have to suck! And there's something they can do about it right now. So join us and The Better Boss Project movement! We're here to coach you individually, consult with your organization, or lead action-packed team-building activities. If you want to go deeper on any of The Better Boss Blueprint principles, we've got a whole company with insightful, simple, and memorable resources to support you. Join us in striving to Live and Lead with #NoRegrets!

(Contact us at noregrets@thebetterbossproject.com)

ACKNOWLEDGMENTS

AS I PUT THE FINISHING touches on this book, I'm in Mumbai, India preparing to work with the local team of one of my global clients. I couldn't be in a more perfect place from which to be scribing my acknowledgements. There's something about the graciousness of the people here and the rich cultural vibe that inspires reflection and gratitude. This book is a long time coming, and there are dozens, if not hundreds, of people to acknowledge for their meaningful roles in my life.

First things first…thank you to my parents, Joel and Carol Duberstein, for their unconditional love and encouragement from the moment I was born. Many of my biggest strengths are attributable to your excellent parenting and role modeling, not the least of which are my passion for writing, emotional intelligence, compassion, and unyielding determination. Mom, I am indebted to you specifically for the excellent job you did editing and proofreading this book (nice try on the milder synonyms to replace the expletives by the way!); you're the best grammarian and wordsmith I've ever met, and sincerely appreciate all your help and guidance. Also, thank you Mom and Dad for my younger sister Nanci, who gave me the two best nephews an aunt could ever want in Aidan and Kyle.

Immeasurable gratitude to Alan for remembering my phone number in 1992, for being the first love of my life, and for the invaluable lessons your death taught and continues to teach me and others. You were and still are the epitome of a better boss. And thank you to Alan's amazing family and friends, who have helped keep his memory and spirit vibrantly alive. Mom-in-law Joyce, brother-in-law Marc, sister-in-law Beth, and nephews Adam and Ben never stopped being family. Marc, who knew when you recommended Vail for my first ski trip out west that I'd end up living there one day?!

Thank you to Brad Magosky for teaching me how to ride a motorcycle and being my fellow adrenaline junkie. You're also a great co-parent to our cat babies, Elaine and Kramer. I adore your generous family and can't believe I was ever intimidated to meet your six sisters (and three brothers!) at my first Thanksgiving with your loving clan.

Of course, I want to thank all the bosses I've ever had, both great and not so great, as each of you helped shape who I am and what I believe professionally. In particular, thank you to Goldman Sachs for the crucial formative influence you had and high standards you instilled. And thank you to everyone who has ever worked for me, directly or indirectly, from the A+ performers to those I terminated. You all taught me valuable lessons.

I'm also grateful for the many extracurricular influences throughout my life. Most recently, I had the privilege of being a member of a very special "tribe" of 28 leaders as part of CTI's Co-Active® Leadership Program. My definition of leadership has been permanently expanded, as has the remarkable new range of ways to demonstrate it. I couldn't have hand-picked better co-facilitators for our tribe of "Crocodiles," whose name was inspired by our characteristic strength, creativity, instinctual gifts, and collective fierceness—fierce in a good way. L.A. Redding, the rare example you set of tremendously bold yet equally caring leadership is a constant source of inspiration and reminds me to truly embrace my own "danger" type. Art Shirk, like Alan, you departed this world too soon! But not before leaving an indelible imprint on everyone who ever met you and demonstrating what it's like to live and die with grace and without regret. To my October 1st birthday sister, Kim Smolik, thank you for your collaboration, never-ending willingness to provide valuable feedback, and most importantly, devoted friendship. Limitless gratitude also envelops the whole tribe for impressing on me in real-time that I'm most compelling as a leader when I check in with my heart in addition to my often-over-relied-upon head.

In no particular order, other vital—and some random—acknowledgements go out to:

› My clients. You're the best and it's a privilege to work with you all.
› The close friends I've collected over the years who are like sisters and brothers to me. From the years growing up in Savannah, GA to present times, you know who you are and I love you.
› The various coaches I have worked with over the years, including Jodie Morrow, Adam Reynolds, Meryl Martin, and Pat Carrington-House. Thank you for helping me hone in on what I wanted, even when it was murky, and process the myriad ups-and-downs of life and career.

- Author and blogger Seth Godin for teaching us that "Purple Cows" are good and for inspiring me to speak authentically to my "tribe."
- Author Elizabeth Gilbert for sharing her wisdom on "Big Magic," which propelled me to FINALLY write parts of my story.
- Writer Anne Lamott for coining the phrase "shitty first draft" and insisting that "all good writers write them."
- Esbe van Heerden for project managing the book's design, editing and proofreading. You were an absolute joy to work with!
- The awesome team at my media relationships firm, Poston Communications. Here's to the past five years of partnership and many more!
- Jim Handel, the former Chase Manhattan VP who hired me out of college into the bank's prestigious Management Development Program in New York City even though he'd been sent to Miami to recruit a Spanish speaker…y solo hablo un poquito de español.
- Mayor Rudi Giuliani for cleaning up NYC. There's no place I'd rather have lived in my 20s.
- Yoga teacher Bryan Kest for proving that one can curse and be spiritual at the same time.
- Parade Magazine for sponsoring the national essay contest in which I won first place in 9th grade. The prize of two-weeks in Italy and (former) Yugoslavia set in motion a wanderlust that has defined me ever since.
- Coaches Howard Schnellenberger and Jimmy Johnson for building the University of Miami Hurricane's football team into a dynasty. Because of you and the excellent education I received at "The U," I bleed orange and green.
- The Universe, for wide-ranging inspiration in so many forms.

As you well know by now, I try my best to Live and Lead with #NoRegrets and encourage others to do the same. And one of the best ways to do that is to Live and Lead with #gratitude. Thank you!

ABOUT THE AUTHOR

McKinsey-style expertise, IKEA-like simplicity, and Jon Stewart-esque irreverence is what you get with leadership development consultant Shani Magosky. She founded The Better Boss Project based on years of experience working with leaders at all levels and a desire to change organizations by helping people become better bosses – of others and themselves. Previously, she worked in three divisions of Goldman Sachs, managed a TV station, and was COO of an all-virtual international marketing company. She counsels a range of Fortune 1000 companies, startups, entrepreneurs, universities, and non-profits across multiple industries. In addition to decades of hard-earned corporate leadership stripes, Shani is also a Professional Certified Coach (PCC) with the International Coach Federation (ICF), certified practitioner of the Leadership Circle 360 Profile and Leadership Culture Survey, and graduate of the Co-Active® Leadership Program. In her free time, you'll find Shani rock climbing, practicing yoga, hurtling down black diamond ski slopes, riding her Harley, or watching Miami Hurricanes football games. She can be reached at shani@thebetterbossproject.com.